It's All in the Sharing

Credits

Front and Back Cover - Carmen Marrero

Author Photo – Jason Hahn

Editing – John Reeser & Pedro Ochoa

2nd Edition

SEATTLE
LIFE COACH TRAINING
train to transform lives

It's All in the Sharing

If you don't go within, you go without

Richard Seaman
Master Life Coach
www.seattlelifecoachtraining.com

In the sharing is where it begins.
In the sharing is where the first light flickers
within the unconscious mind. If I am the flicker
of light to one person who is asleep to their own
potential, than my life was never in vain.

This book is dedicated to my mother, Sandra, and anyone who was told they couldn't...

It's Not True – You Can.

Acknowledgments

First and foremost, my deepest gratitude to God, my higher power for making this possible. Thank you for moving through me and inspiring me to listen to your whispers within me. Thank you for the 4 a.m. wake up calls to get me up to write.

To my birth mom, Sandi, thank you for always encouraging me. Thank you for continually telling me how proud you are of me. Thank you for raising me to be the man I have become. I am so proud you are my mom. Thank you for always loving me unconditionally.

To my spiritual mom, Gabriele, who would sit with me for countless hours on the phone encouraging me to write. Thank you for the many teachings you shared with me. Your passion and enthusiasm for life are what kept me going even when I wanted to give up. Thank you for believing in me.

To the woman that helped me realize my greatness, KC Miller, words cannot express my gratitude and appreciation for what you have done for me. You saw my gifts even when I couldn't. You held my arms up when I was weak. You pushed me out in front of an audience to speak even when I was terrified. You helped me realize there is power in my speaking. You gave me a platform and showed me my purpose in life. Thank you for listening to God and doing your dream. You have touched so many lives because you listened. I am in Awe of you.

To Linda Bennett, my teacher, my friend. Thank you for sitting with me and listening to me on so many levels. Thank you for believing in me and giving me so many opportunities to shine bright. Thank you for being there for me at my darkest hours and helping me realize I deserve to have a partner and not a project. Thank you for helping me see the "spam" in my life as a good thing.

To my dog, Harpo, who is the smartest Jack-Russell Terrier in the world. Thank you for lying at my feet night after night as I wrote this book. Thank you for being my longest and most loyal companion. Your intuitiveness to read me has always been my rock, which kept me grounded in this world. You were a gift from God and I will always cherish our unique relationship.

To my clients and students. You have taught me so much. I received back more than you can imagine. You allowed me to teach and coach you, which gave me my purpose in this life. I look forward to many more years of living my purpose.

To all those random editors out there who were brave enough to let me know when something needed attention. Words cannot express my heartfelt thanks to you. You helped me stay passionate by continually encouraging me with your suggestions. You became a part of the energy of this book. Thank you for all your hard work.

To Carmen Marrero, the work you did on the book is fabulous and your energy will always be in the book.

To my friends and family who contributed in their own way, there are so many thanks I have for all of you. You know who you are. Many blessings.

CONTENTS

SLCT

train to transform lives
www.seattlelifecoachtraining.com

Foreword

Everyone has stories. In fact, most of our everyday conversations are filled with the telling of little stories here and there about things happening to us or around us. The great teachers throughout history have used stories and parables to illustrate deep spiritual concepts. Stories are our life.

The concern or challenge comes when we get stuck in our stories. These stories become the place we hide; the place we live and the place part of us dies.

The author of this powerful book you are holding is a 'Man of Power'. What you will come to know and love about Richard is his stories are transformational teaching tools. He shares, we grow – it is his gift.

One of Richard's strengths is he is a Story-Buster. You have heard of a Ghost-buster - someone who comes in, chases the haunting's from the past away, creating a new fresh space for people to live. The ghost-busting process is not always gentle, however, it is effective. That's Richard. I have watched Richard lovingly listen to a person's story in the most active and engaged way, wait, and then pose a question that literally propels the person into a new dimension. When this happens, the ghosts of past stories are extricated and entanglements from the past are unraveled. Richard has the ability to do this because he has stood up to his own ghosts. He has faced the gremlins and gargoyles - those ugly little buggers with big mouths, with hurtful things coming out of them. He stands as a champion today. Richard shares his stories; he brings them to the foot of the cross and offers them up to God for revelation and transformation.

One day Richard came into my office with a very heavy heart and equally sad story. "My heart hurts for a student in one of my classes who chooses to hang on to his story of brokenness, rather than exchange it for a story of greatness - of breakthrough - of transformation," Richard shared while holding his hands to his chest. "How do we reach him?" was Richard's plea, as much to God as he was asking it of me. After a long silence, he said, "This is when I know I need to share my stories - to create recognition and motivation, not pity and emotional poverty. I will not wallow in my stories. I will find the wisdom and walk into my greatness from them." At that moment I realized I had witnessed a miracle. In the same way he creates clarity for others, he experienced a shift in perception for himself – he went from wondering to knowing his destined path.

The sharing of a story can be divine intercession, rearranging our perceptions of an event resulting in rearranging the way we show up in the world. It's all in the intention of the sharing.

Richard is a Masterful Transformational Life Coach, as well as a Master Toe Reader. A Toe Reader is someone who honors the stories coded in the toes and is spiritually and emotionally available to unlock the storyline stored in the cells of the body, specifically stored in the hologram of the toes. In chapter seven he shares one my favorite toe reading stories about surrendering to Spirit and being used as God's reset button for people who are stuck in their stories because of their fear.

Richard has asked the question of Spirit: "What are the ways in which I can serve?" This book is one of the answers to his question.

Blessings,
KC Miller
Author of Toe Reading - Are You Walking Your Destined Path?
Founder of Southwest Institute of Healing Arts

It's All in the Sharing

"If you don't go within, you go without"

Richard Seaman

Master Life Coach

PREFACE

My goal is to write a book that will allow my words, thoughts and sharing to move you forward into the life you deserve. My intention for this book is to add value to your life, leaving you with tools, skills, abundance, joy and peace after each chapter. I would like for you to bubble over in gratitude and allow this book to transform your life. My hope would be when you read the words on these pages you might say to yourself, "Huh, I never thought of it that way."

The intention I am working from would hopefully play out like this: I am here to teach you in a spiritual way that will empower you to know yourself and God in powerful ways, and when you think of God you will be open to receive all of the abundance He has for your life. May you know there is enough for everyone and digging in the garbage for sustenance is not necessary nor is it part of the plan for you. There is always enough and God is supporting you all the time.

If there is sin, the Course of Miracles says, sin could be defined as the perception we are separated from self and/or we are separated from our Creator. The truth is we are always connected and always being supported all the time by our Higher Power.

Each person has their own timeline and will experience their "Awe Ha's" in perfect timing. God is perfectly on time and never late.

As I write I start to see myself come alive in anticipation of what is before me, much like the joy and high of starting a new job. My experience, wisdom, joy, hurt, pain and knowledge is being written down and recorded in hopes it will become a tool for another person to break-through the fear and obstacles keeping them stuck and revolving back to what they know. Do you want to revolve or evolve?

It's all in the sharing. This is where it starts. In the sharing is where everything becomes possible. In the sharing is where the first light flickers within the unconscious mind. If I can be a flicker of light to one person who is asleep to their own potential then my life is not in vain. Are you ready to receive all that God has to offer you? Are you ready to enrich your life?

If you don't go within, you go without.

Blessings,
    ~ Richard Seaman

Allegorical Introduction

Free to Be

Love is two pillars standing side by side with the wind blowing between them.

Two men ventured to the top of a great, snow covered mountain; the time spent together ushered in conversation, about their theories, beliefs and ideas each held regarding relationships. As they traveled towards the white magnificent mountain it grew larger and larger, all the more grandeur in their sight. As they ventured up a very steep, windy road they spoke about their experiences and philosophies of relationships they've had, and they came to conclude that neither one had a transparent paradigm as to what a true relationship was supposed to be; especially romantic relationships.

Arriving at the mountain top many hours later, the men found that the snow covered ground reflected the sun's light to such a degree that it was blinding them to see clearly. With no way to filter out the sun's passionate force, they constructed make-shift head covers using their sweaters. Wrapping the sweaters around their heads in such a way that it created small peek-a-boo openings to see from. With one mans vision impaired, the other man guided him through the snow until the men soon became frustrated. The man guiding suggested they move into the forest, where they would be protected from the sun by the canopy of trees.

Stepping into the shade of the trees, the men's' frustration seemed to dissolve as they felt the protection of the green canopy above them. A sense of freedom and comfort came over them, and they both agreed they were grateful to be out of the sun's intense, blinding rays. Taking in a deep breath, the once frustrated men allowed their eyes to adjust to the serenity of the forest in front of them, and all around them.

Enveloped by the coolness and calmness of the forest, the men began to walk aimlessly further into the woods. They began to walk without expectation and allowed themselves to get lost in the mystical environment that enveloped them. Each step drew them deeper into the dense forest, and soon calmness fell over them. The deeper they went into the woods the further they wanted to explore. They were feeling no sense of obligation, just the freedom to be in the moment, recognizing the wonder without having to talk about it. Gradually stillness came over the two men and they stopped walking and became very still and quiet. They stood in the middle of the forest, surrounded by the deep intensity of the green canopy overhead and listened to the silence of the moment.

Overhead they noticed a flock of birds flittering around in the trees. They seemed so free, so happy, so excited about something. The men began to raise their arms up toward the trees to point out the birds to each other. As they did a few of the birds glided down to get a closer look at the men. Their personal space was tested momentarily. They were almost too close for comfort, as though they wanted something from them and the men were feeling a little hesitant. Neither one had ever experienced wild birds coming that close. These particular birds seemed to be very engaged and began to swirl above their head and arms. They were getting close enough to see their eyes and feet and the special markings on their feathers. The men were entranced by their behavior and felt a rush of adrenaline at the newness of this experience.

Then, the birds departed as quickly as they arrived. The men continued to gaze upward at the beauty of the overhead canopy and the foreign world of various, enormous wise trees surrounding and encircling them. The deeper they went into the woods, the further they wanted to explore. As they ventured further through this magical northwest forest they continued to hear the flutter of wings and then spotted a flock of colorful, majestic birds perched above them high, high in the treetops.

All at once, a knowing came over the men and they raised their hands to expose their palms. Holding their arms up, palms open, a single bird swooped down and landed directly onto one mans open hand. He was stunned and surprised and even a little scared fearing this bird may become aggressive. The other man watching yelled from across the clearing. "Don't move; just stand there with your hands open." He did and within seconds another bird landed on his other hand. He just stood there as quietly as he could and waited to see what would happen. He dropped his hands slightly to get a clearer view of the birds. He looked into their eyes and they looked into his. They were all very interested in each other.

He began to notice the calmer he was the more comfortable the birds seemed to become. They began to walk back and forth from his hands to his forearms and then back to his hands. They seemed to sit and analyze him with a look of some sort of admiration. Then suddenly, one of the birds flew off and into the security of the treetops. The other bird followed immediately behind. He knew something spectacular had just happened.

He wanted more. He lifted his arms and exposed the palms of his hands to the trees again, waiting for the birds to come back. Within seconds he saw the birds begin to rustle and fly out of the trees. Perhaps they were looking for a safe place to land. Again they landed directly onto his open hand. But this time it was with a more confident landing. He seemed to be a safe place for the birds to land.

His friend was now sitting on a rock nearby coaching him to be calm and keep his hands open. He told him not to tug, pull or make any sudden movements. He began to notice many more birds above, flying, swooping and watching their bird friends and the men as if they might be wondering what they might have to offer them.   With arms up and hands open he remained calm. Another bird landed and then another, and another. Five birds had landed on his arms and hands using him as a perch - a resting place. He had become a safe place to land. They could come and go as they wanted. There was no tugging, pulling or harassing. It was just a safe place for them to come and go without expectation or attachment to the outcome. There was nothing to fear. It was a safe place to be.

He allowed the birds to move around his body as they pleased. They seemed to be enjoying their new playground. He was in such awe of their trust he didn't want the moment to end. But, then the birds quickly flew away once again into the treetops.

Standing very still, both men inhaled the beauty by closing their eyes. They both reached their arms and hands upward into the sky, and as they did a peace, serenity and calmness permeated every cell of their body. As the men stood upright, arms up, palms out and open, making a universal jester to receive more. They began to hear the sound of bird's wings flutter above them again, as if there was some sort of rally starting to take place in the trees.

Then, the other man felt the sudden thud on the palm of his hand. Slowly he opened his eyes to find a pair of beautiful dark blue eyes staring back at him. The bird pulled its head back and seemed to be smiling at the man and gradually moved in closer. Feeling the comfort and peace in the man's face, the bird felt at ease and moved about the man. Running up and down the man's arms all the way to his shoulder, the bird seemed to be using the man as a playground. Suddenly, the man heard a voice, "Love is two pillars standing side by side, with the wind blowing between them." Bewildered, he jumped causing the bird to fly away. He gazed into the direction of his friend only to find him standing still with his arms up, palms open, stretching himself into the sky.

Relaxing once again the man reached up to the sky but detained himself from closing his eyes this time around. To his surprise, another bird flew down and landed squarely in the palm of his hand. Lowering his hand to the level of his eyes, the man's gaze fell upon a strikingly awkward colored bird; its feathers every hue of red imaginable. The bird opened its beak, but instead of a chirp the man heard the fluid sound of words escaping through the bird's breath.

"A pillar is designed to support weight. Just as the pillar, you are designed to support the weight and stress of being human. Don't be afraid to trust in the pillar inside of you. You were designed to be an instrument of peace. Your pillar is God. When you love someone you allow them to be free to be how they choose to be. Each pillar knows where it begins and ends, and if those pillars come too close together the structure they are holding up will eventually come tumbling down. Love is not co-dependent; love is inter-dependent. You do not loose yourself in love, you find yourself."

No longer stunned by the talkative birds, the man just listened as several birds came on to him and spoke. Landing inches from his ear, a yellow feathered bird whispered "Be a resting place; a safe place to land." Then, a blue-green, shimmering feathered bird landed and gazed into his eyes. Opening its beak it said, "Do not tug, pull or harass; come and go without expectation or attachment to the outcome." Another bird with feathers of green and gold said "You can't take someone else's free will."

The man began to realize that each bird was a truth bringer and a great wise messenger who has come to teach him about relationships. The magical birds frolicked all over him and after a while the birds flew back into the trees. He had a sense of freedom overcome him as he watched all but one bird flutter up into the air.

This bird was a pure white dove that planted himself directly on the man's palm. He lifted the dove closer to his face and as their eyes met, the bird spoke with the softest, clearest and most truthful voice the man had ever heard before.

"Just as you were blinded by the sun's reflection of the snow, you are also blinded to the idea of how to have healthy relationships. Many books have been written to enlighten you humans on how to develop healthy relationships. But, what we, the birds, have shared with you today about healthy, respectful relationships will be far more enlightening than any book could ever be. You cannot take away someone else's free will. In fact, in the bible it's says, 'God would never take away your free will. You will always have your free will.' In most relationships, the players take certain roles. Some people are controlling, some are rescuers and some are doormats. When your relationships have high drama or chaos or when one party is very self-righteous or judgmental you tend to feel unsafe. We the birds taught you today to approach relationships calmly and openly. You now know to approach without expectation or attachment to the outcome. Let your fear about vulnerability scatter and know that just because you show your vulnerabilities does not mean you lose your creditability. When you release and let go, your relationships will be joyful, peaceful and full of freedom. Learn to love yourself first, fully and completely before you enter into a relationship. Relationships are not here to complete you, they are here to enhance you and support you as you find and share your own higher awareness. When you show up as this higher self, then there is nothing to fear."

The man with the dove looks to his left and sees the other man standing in astonishment of the dove's message. And, as the man makes eye contact with the dove again, the dove winks, flaps its wings and flies away into the sky leaving a tail feather in the man's open palm. This leaves the men with a profound experience, a legendary, timeless lesson on relationships and a tail feather as a reminder.

I want to feel like a bird singing in an open cage. I want to be in love where I am free to wander. I want to lay down with my eyes shut and let the mystic take all of my sadness. If this is what you call love then I am happiness - and so it is.

"Today, God, I now know how to be free as a bird; let my personal mystic remind me I do not need to pull, tug or harass the people I love. I know how to be in relationships that will honor others and myself. I see myself now standing in relationships with other's hands up, palms open, being calm and free. We are free to be. I am free to be. I release this prayer in the law of God as done. And, so it is."

Sharing

"It is a part of our survival"

Sharing is the universal language in which we, as humans, relate to each other through the stories we tell each other. We share our stories with the world in many ways. We do it through TV, media, support groups, school, family, telephone, Internet, books, advertising, business cards and much more. We are always sharing if you just stop to notice. It's the way we are and we cannot help it. We have been given a voice and a language to share with each other. Without sharing our lives we would be incomplete and empty. We all have a story to tell and we all want to share our experience of the world.

Sharing connects us in a unique way - as though someone else is actually witnessing our life experience. Someone else is growing because they relate to our story through empathy and compassion. Some people have had similar experiences; others have traveled another path. We all love to look into someone else's life and we do it through sharing; either theirs or ours.

Television is all about sharing, from reality TV, documentaries, and real life true stories. And, of course, there is the "Queen" of sharing, Oprah. Her entire premise is sharing. She shares back and forth across the world via television. Larry King is another TV personality whose whole program is about sharing.

There are many types of programs on the radio and the TV that could be included in this list of programs where sharing is the primary activity. The biggest Internet sharing systems recently have been Facebook, Linkedin and YouTube, which have taken over the world in a global way. If you look at any person's blog you will see people sharing who they are. Internet sharing has become a new norm in our society and a means to share who we are, what we like and what we are looking for.

Look around and notice that we as human beings have this burning need to share our lives with people we come into contact with. It has become a part of our survival. As a life coach that has guided thousands of people to a more powerful life, one of the things I do most in my practice is sit with people and listen to them share their lives with me. There seems to be magic when two or more people are gathered together to share themselves. I have witnessed this countless times and I know the power of sharing. My hope for you is as you continue to read this book you will see my sharing as a reflection of your life. There may be a piece of you inside these pages. Enjoy what I have birthed. If you don't go within, you go without.

God's Job

"Who better to do God's job than God?"

When you step in and do God's job you cripple everyone involved. The person you are trying to help is hearing you say, "You're not doing a good enough job in your life. So let me do it for you." Didn't God give everyone free will? Who are you to take away free choice or even suggest another way of being, especially if the person never asked you for your opinion?

Treating people like they are big enough are capable, and they know what is best for them, creates the best and fastest results. Everyone walks their own unique path, doing their own unique things. Different is a good thing. A garden needs balance to be in harmony. Different types of flowers, trees, and cactus are needed to create the perfect landscape.

Let us help each person to create their own personal niche in life, especially if their life is different from yours. Walk away from the fear in your heart about differences and the unknown. Let go of the unhealthy ego that tells you you're better than others. Embrace the amazing totality of God everywhere and see His harmony in everything.

When you treat others like there is something lacking in them, you are really saying you don't trust God. If you did you would already know God is in control. God is in charge of life and the universe.

I live for God and God has my back. My life is under control. God works within me in His timeline. Not yours. There are three types of business: your business, someone else's business and God's business.

When you want to fix someone or have comments about someone else's life, direct those concerns to God through prayer. Let us pray for those whom we have concern for, however let us never force our will onto others, especially when they never asked us in the first place.

"Today, God, help me to be strong enough to not rescue or fix. Allow me to allow others to walk with you in peace. I know my will is only that - my will. I release this prayer into the truth of the law of God to be done. And, so it is."

Seekers vs. Non-Seekers

*"Every moment we have a choice to choose
the light or the darkness"*

There are two types of people in this life:
Seekers and Non-seekers. Seekers are people
who love the truth and the light. Non-seekers
are people who run from the truth at any cost
because they're afraid of the truth and how it
may reflect on them. When you are run down
and feel as though you have nothing left,
seeking the truth will guide you to the light
where you can recharge and energize yourself.

The reason you are run down and
exhausted from your everyday life may be
because you are focusing on darkness. Lies
come from darkness and the darkness only has
one purpose. The purpose of darkness is to
draw us in, drain our energy and make our lives
hard.

If you are feeling run down, ask yourself if
you have been drawn into the darkness of lies.
These lies may be the lies of others or they may
be your own. If you feel as if your soul is dying,
move into the light. The light will always

overpower the darkness. Darkness and negativity cannot live in the light and when the truth of the light appears through the mist of darkness, darkness flees like a coward because it can't stand anything that is good.

There is power in knowledge. The more you move into the truth and knowledge the stronger you will get. The stronger your light shines, the quicker the negativity that is harassing you will flee. The darkness hates the light and the truth. Darkness cannot hide when the light appears. The more you continue to feed into evil's harassment by talking about it or allowing it to stress you out, it wins, and the darkness will envelop you until you lie down and say "Kill me, I can't stand it anymore."

I know you are a seeker of truth. Perhaps you have forgotten who you are or veered off your path of becoming the best you can be. You want love just like everyone else does in this life. Many of us have done things for love that were not in our best and highest good. Many of us have a story of destruction, too. There is a masterpiece within all of us. It just takes a lot of chipping away at all the outside marble to find it. Chip away my friend, chip away.

"Today, God, help me to remember who I am and who I came here to be in this world. I am a seeker of the truth and the light. I now

know when I am in a negative place in my life I can always make another choice to return to a place of power and light. I can move in the flow of good. I release this prayer into the law of God as done. And, so it is."

Claim Your Greatness

"It is not ego, It is our divine calling,
It is our right to claim our greatness"

In 1988, Oprah claimed her greatness to the world on a Barbara Walters special. She said, "I have always known I was destined to do great things." The public ridiculed her for what she said. They thought she was coming from ego. How dare a black woman claim she was born for greatness? After the nationally televised program, Oprah received many letters telling her she had stepped over the line.

In 2004, Oprah wanted to explain what she had meant. She explained that she believes claiming our greatness is our right. She believes every soul has his/ her calling and every person is destined for greatness. It is our job to discover our destiny while on the earth; the constant tugging and pulling and negativity of this world can distract some people. Some of us have been told we should never shine too brightly. Who are we not to shine brightly and loudly? And, when we do shine brightly there is someone there telling us to dim our lights so we won't make other people uncomfortable. Playing small does not serve the world. When we shine brightly it gives other people permission to do the same.

What if you could find a place where you were asked daily to claim your greatness? Imagine a world so evolved; where we are encouraged by each other to claim our greatness and to raise our vibrations to such a level we could only see each other's gifts, not our downfalls. Imagine a world where we actually empower the people around us to move and grow and expand to their full potential.

I do know of a place just like this. I do know of a place that encourages you to play big and to find your voice and to evolve into the person God wants you to be. I do know of a place that asks you to "Claim your greatness" and to show the world just how big you are. The place is a spirit-directed school in Tempe, AZ. KC Miller, the founder and director of the school, perfects the title of "Instrument of Spirit". KC is someone who claims her greatness just through her being. She is dyslexic and the learning disability doesn't seem to bring her down. She looks at herself as an instrument for God in every moment. She is committed to touching as many lives as she can; helping them discover their gifts and graces in this world. She believes each of us has a destiny and we each have unique gifts and talents. However, sometimes these gifts are not as obvious as we would like them to be.

KC Miller invites people to ask themselves, "How may I best serve? How may I serve the world in a way my daily contribution can make a difference to the overall effort and satisfaction of this world?" As Marianne Williamson says in her book, Return to Love, "Our deepest fear is not that we are inadequate, our deepest fear is that we are powerful beyond measure. It is our light, not our darkness, that frightens us most."

As you discover your gifts and claim your greatness, one of your graces will be to step into your light and be all you can be. May you find your gifts and claim your greatness to the world. It is your privilege, it is your right, and it is your life. You have one life one time. What are you going to do with it?

"Today, God, help me see my greatness. Help me claim to the world my gifts and talents without shame. I am here as your vehicle to be God in action. I am your hands, ears and voice to do your work as a gifted and talented soul on this earth plane. I am full and complete and there is nothing lacking within me. I am ready now to move into my greatness in a powerful and magnificent way today and everyday. I say "YES" to this as truth in my life and know I am always empowered by God and his angels. I

release this prayer into the law of God as done.
And, so it is."

Finding Your Purpose

> "Just as 'A' is the first letter in the alphabet,
> awareness is the first step to
> health and healing"

To make changes in your life you have to wake up to the awareness that you are not living fully to your potential. To experience life fully is to realize your life purpose or calling - the reason we are here on earth.

We ask ourselves at times, "Why am I here"? And, some of us don't know how to answer the question. In Richard Bach's book, Illusions he says, "Here is a test whether or not your mission in life is finished. If we are alive it isn't".

One way to find your mission in life is to become aware of when you feel blissful. Do you remember a time when you were doing something for many hours and when you looked at the clock you realized time had just passed by. The place you were in was bliss. Time does not exist when we are in a blissful state.

To find your bliss ask yourself, where does time not exist? This is where you belong. Bliss is where you will find yourself and the reason and mission of your life. Listen for it by becoming aware of the loss of time.

Try new things that show up in your life. If you always go back to what you know you will never expand enough to find your bliss. There is always something you can create to help find bliss. Take a risk and move out of your comfort zone. Become aware of what types of things you are attracted to. Move toward those things and start doing them and watch yourself become alive with a constant stream of endurance and abundance that is going directly into what you are creating. At this moment you are co-creating with God and His purpose for you on earth. Become a doer of what you do really well and what comes naturally to you. When you realize what you're doing is enjoyable and you don't mind putting forth the effort to do it because it seems effortless, then you are in your bliss. You are in effortless being.

"Today, God, help me find my bliss and my purpose in life. I know when I am happy I am glorifying you and your will for my life and then I am in my purpose. May I walk into my life aware of each footstep I take. May I take one step at a time into my life's purpose. My bliss. You are calling me by name. I give thanks for

the knowledge I am worthy of a purpose and the timeless void of bliss. I release this prayer into God's law as done. And, so it is."

Now

"Right now is all there is, everything
else is an illusion"

Throughout the years many writers have
written about the concept of "Now". There are
many ideas of what the power of now is.

Move through your day believing you are
right where you are supposed to be at any given
moment. You follow the intent and direction
God wants for you. God has given you the vision
of your life and if you just stop for a moment and
reflect, you will remember a time when you had
this knowing revealed to you. The knowing was
God showing you a vision. This vision may be
revealed to you through a thought, another
person's words, a book, a movie, a song or in a
multitude of ways. The knowing is within you.
You know it, now how do you master it?

Take on one task at a time. Follow God's
path and allow God to create your future. Speak
your intention out loud. Intention is everything.
Without intention we are wandering around
without a plan. Ask God to help you be of
service. "How may I serve today? I say yes to my

life today." Be grateful for this experience to be alive and enjoy this moment.

Time slips away very quickly and then it becomes your past. Ahead of you is the future. The past is slipping away as quickly as your future arrives. Both the future and the past are moving fully present at the same time. It is time overlapping time, moving through you and in you. When we are all living in the now you will be in complete awareness, as a fully realized being. This is all you have and you should be grateful for this moment of now.

When you serve others in the now you are the hands, ears, feet and voice creating new evolving thoughts and concepts. Being in the now is the only place that is real.

Ride the moment of now by catching the momentum like you are catching a wave in the ocean. Let it guide you like gravity guides the tides. The pull and tug of the current is God riding you like a jockey rides a thoroughbred racing horse. The jockey guides the horse through pulling, tugging, plowing and using certain amounts of pressure. Let God ride you in the race of your life. Run like the wind, kick up your heels, lift your tail and let your mane flap in the wind.

Living in the now and allowing God to create your day involves letting go and letting

God and can be almost effortless. When you put yourself in neutral and wait on God's whispers within you, he will tug on your heart and move you in a certain direction. When you listen close to the whispers, it will remind you of who you are and who you have come here to be.

Have you ever taken a vacation where everything was planned? You knew what time you would arrive, where you were going to eat, all the activities you were going to do. There was a sense of social obligation and there was no freedom to just be impulsive and allow the day to unfold. Those types of trips can be frustrating because something may have tugged on you, begging you to step out of your planned agenda. You may have been standing on a street corner and noticed something down the street that looked really fun or inviting. But, because you already had everything planned for the day and were socially obligated you felt like you couldn't do what your heart wanted to do.

The best trips you can take are the ones where nothing is preplanned. All you know is the destination, when you are going to leave and when you will return. Everything else in between is up to spirit to guide you and ride you through those trips. See yourself as a leaf in the wind, and you will find those trips to be the most rewarding and fulfilling.

A previous client once took a nine-day cruise to the Mexican Riviera. Each day he would awaken with no expectations. He never knew what he would feel like doing that day. He remained open to whatever the universe had in store for him. He reported the vacation was amazing and everything he needed. He was spontaneous and in the moment of now. When he returned home he found there was completeness within himself and he had no regrets.

The power is in the now. Now is all you have. You can forecast the future and have goals to achieve, but ultimately it's up to God. I remember a story I heard one day on the local news that put it all into perspective. There was a bus full of people. I am sure each person woke up in the morning with a plan; places to go and things to achieve for the day. Well, none of those passengers with a plan made it to their destinations. The bus was hijacked by a gun-slinging madman. Just as the bus was traveling over a bridge, this man shot the bus driver sending the bus flying off the bridge onto an apartment complex below. Many people in the bus died including the bus driver and the man that hijacked the bus. Some of the people below were also hurt and killed and their plans for the day were thwarted.

This story is a perfect example of the importance of living in the now. Of course we have places to be and things to do. But, if God wants to change those plans He does in an instant. When we release, let go and let God we are allowing Spirit to move through us and to create our day. Tragic events happen everyday. There is a reason for them. The best thing we can do is go with the flow and know there is a reason even if we do not understand what the reason is.

"Today, God, help me to understand the things that do not make sense to me. I want to live in the now and let go of all my worries about the future. I know when I lay awake at night worrying about my past or my future that I am not living in the now. I know when I let go I will know. I release this prayer into the law of God as done. And, so it is."

Orbs

"It is only our fear that stops us
from believing"

My grandmother, Delores, or as we called her, Nana, was very near and dear to my heart. When I was young I used to sit at her kitchen table looking out into the front yard. Nana's favorite pastime was to sit at the table and drink coffee. We had many hours of fun at the table playing card games and sharing many dinners she cooked for us. The kitchen was the energy hub of the house and was where everyone preferred to be.

I used to sit there with her and we would talk about the supernatural, ghosts and spirits. My grandmother was very psychic and had the ability to read the energy from the cup you were drinking from. In fact, I learned not to leave my coffee cup on the table when I left the room, because if I did, she would pick it up and read my energy and end up knowing pretty much everything she wanted to know. When I came back she began firing questions at me; prying and wanting to know more about my life.

Throughout the years Nana and I both knew I was developing my abilities as an intuitive and psychic. She was really the only one I could talk to about my "knowing." She always understood me and told me to be very careful and protect myself from evil things that might want to attack me. Her warnings scared me because I had seen the classic movie, The Exorcist and I didn't want anything to do with that kind of evil. I began to believe this "gift" was from the devil and I should not use it. I refused it and denied it most of my life. I pushed aside the stream of constant information I received, denying my "gift" out of sheer fear.

One of the conversations I constantly had with my grandmother was if one of us died before the other, we would do whatever it took to give the other one a sign we were ok and that there is life on the "other side." We both promised each other multiple times we would do whatever we could to contact each other.

On September 28th, 2005 my Nana passed away peacefully in her own home surrounded by her family. I remember the night she died. It was a beautiful passing; filled with much love and dignity. I was of course hurt and crying because I knew I was going to miss her very much. She was always there for me. She understood me and never judged me. She was my safe haven and without her in my life I would not be the same person.

Much earlier that night I decided to go back to my mom's house, which was very close to Nana's. I decided to keep the phone close to me in case someone called in the night to tell me she had passed. I was in a deep sleep when suddenly I was awakened by what seemed to be a large, flying entity above me. It was quick and fierce with a high amount of a wind and pressure and it flew right above me. I quickly sat up and I knew instantly Nana was gone. Within just a few seconds my cell phone began to ring. It was my mom. "Rich, she's gone, honey." "Ok, I will be there in a few minutes," I replied.

The mortuary was called to come and pick up her body. When they arrived it felt very odd to have these complete strangers coming into the house to get my Nana's body. Just before the men were going to bring her out, zipped up in a bag and lying on a stretcher on wheels, they shouted out to the family, "Ok, we are bringing her out now." Everyone ran into the kitchen so as not to have to see her in a body bag. I, however decided to sit in the living room and watch her being wheeled out of her bedroom, through the living room directly past me. Out the door she went and so did I. I followed her body all the way to the white van parked out on the sidewalk. They opened up the double doors on the back of the van and slid her in and shut the doors.

It was 5:20 am and the sun was just beginning to perk up slightly and there were a few birds rustling in the trees above. I could see my breath as I exhaled. Tears were rolling down my cheeks and almost immediately they turned cold from the fall-frosted coldness in the air. The men got into the van, started the engine and began pulling away. I stood there quietly watching the taillights move farther away until they turned right and disappeared. "Goodbye Nana, I love you. Don't forget about me."

In January of 2006 I moved into my new home in south Phoenix. It was a big deal for me because it was the first time I had achieved home ownership. I had always wanted to own my own home and I finally accomplished that goal. I had some landscaping work done in the backyard. A company came and installed curbing creating a border for more landscaping.

I was on the phone one night with my mom. I was telling her about the curbing. She said she wished she could see it. I explained to her, "We'll, you can. Let me take a digital picture of it while I am on the phone with you and I will email it to you right now."

As I was taking the pictures and talking to mom, I mentioned I wished Nana could see my house. Mom said, "Oh, I am sure she can see it." After I had snapped several shots I went in and downloaded the pictures directly onto the computer. As they came up I began to notice strange lights in the pictures. Circles of light in many different places throughout the photos. There was one particularly amazing one. It was a single giant orb of light with girth, depth and form. It hovered two feet off the ground and seemed to be directly in front of the block wall.

I sent the pictures to my mom and we were both completely stunned. We believed I had just attracted this amazing energy and this was validation there is life on the other side. I believe this was my Nana and she was giving me a sign she can see me and she is fine.

After the first set of photos, orbs began appearing in many, many more of the pictures I would take. I have archived hundreds of photos in the past two years. After the giant orb showed up in my back- yard, orbs just continued to present themselves. It was like a porthole was opened for flow between dimensions and the space we shared.

About a year later I was asked to go to a holistic gathering in Chicago called "Celebrate Your Life". I am a Certified Toe Reader and I teach at the school that created toe reading as a healing modality. This was my second year as a toe reader at this conference. We were scheduled to read for three days in different time slots. The crowd of people really enjoyed the readings and there was always a line of people waiting to have their toes read. The soles of the foot and the toes have a story to tell, about your past and your future. The toes can tell us if you procrastinate or if you really get things done. Toe readers sit and ask you deep and probing questions about your life. We will sit and cry with you. I am humbled by the greatness of people's toes and in awe of how amazing they truly are. It was a fun and low-keyed three days.

Saturday night I went to dinner with my fellow toe readers and we shared our day with each other as we refueled our bodies with food. Being around such evolved and spiritually enlightened people gives normal chitchat an entirely new face. A usual topic of choice might be "How are you playing small in the world?" That happened to be the topic at this evening's meal. "How are we playing small in the world?" was asked of me first. I passed and asked to share last. The question was asked of each of us that night. As one of my friends was answering the question, I heard Spirit say very clearly to me, "That is your question." My friend's answer to the question was this: "I am playing small with my gift of medium ship."

As she answered the question I began to have an internal dialog with God. I heard my friend's answer echoed back to me. When will I realize my true gift of medium ship and use it for God's purposes? When I get information like that it comes to me in a millisecond. I see everything within my mind's eye in a flash. I spoke back to God, "Ok, fine if you want me to use medium ship as one of my gifts then I am willing to be of service for the good of all." We continued to move around the table until everyone, including myself, had answered the question. I publically committed to use my God-given gifts.

Waking up earlier than normal I decided to check out early and head down to the restaurant in the lobby for a nice breakfast and a cup of coffee. I had not really thought much more about what I had claimed at dinner the night before. I sat and enjoyed my omelet and strong coffee, then headed to my toe reading station.

As I approached I could see the line forming for readings. Some people looked like they had been camping there for a long time. The other readers were buzzing around getting their stations ready. I walked over to my station and began to prepare myself for the next six hours of reading people's toes. I put all my things and props on the table next to my cushion, sat down and took a moment to center myself by breathing in deeply and exhaling even deeper. I opened my hands up which signifies I am an open vessel to be used for God's purposes for the greater good of all.
I sat quietly waiting to hear my inner knowing give me the nudge it was time to call my first client.

I looked behind me and motioned for the first person in line. She walked quickly and sat down in the chair in front of me, her bare feet exposed. We introduced ourselves and I began to tell her about her toes, and their meanings based on the theory that each toe stores a section of our life's story. When I moved to her left foot and I touched her water toe, (which is the forth toe, representing her inner relationships), the number 21 flashed through my mind. I asked her, "What have you been holding on to for 21 years that is not serving you anymore?" She stopped and looked down at me and had no answer. She pondered a little bit longer as I held her water toe. In another flash I began to choke and felt like I was drowning in my own saliva. I held myself together and my breathing returned. When I looked up all I could see in my mind's eye was a heavy-set woman wearing an older style muumuu dress with an apron tied around her waist. She was holding a rolling pin and shaking it toward me as though she were chasing me with it. I told my client what I was seeing in my mind's eye. She explained to me, "That is my mom. She died 21 years ago in London by choking on her saliva. I have been holding on to my mother's death for 21 years and cannot find any peace around it. What else do you see?" I shared with her I could see the kitchen her mom was standing in. "Let me describe it to you. The wall behind her has a long counter top with a lime green sink and white cabinets that go high up to the ceiling. The ceiling is very tall. The counter wraps around to the other wall and forms an L shape. There is an icebox on the left wall with a chrome-style 50's dining room set in the corner. The floor seems old and worn and needs to be replaced. Your mother is just standing there in the kitchen shaking the rolling pin at me."

I looked up at my client after sharing the information that was channeled through me. She was crying and had the most intense and genuine smile on her face I have ever seen. She reached down and touched my face. She said, "I have had no peace around my mother's death. Today, I know and I feel she is exactly where she needs to be. She is exactly the way she was when she was here on earth with me. There is no way you could have known any of this information. I thank you so much for allowing your gift of medium ship to save my soul." She pulled a large bill from her purse and placed it into my tip jar before she walked away.

I just sat there stunned, not sure of what had just happened. A flood of thoughts moved through me. "Wow, I just claimed the gift of medium ship last night. I said, 'yes' to it and the first person that sits down today becomes a recipient as I channeled her mother from the other side." I had really become a neutral space for Spirit to move through me, allowing my mind, body and voice to free another human soul. I had just helped a woman find the peace that had been missing for over 21 years.

"God, if that is what you want from me then bring it on. I am ready to receive this gift. Here I stand with arms wide open."

In that moment I felt reborn with a gift I thought only other people could receive. I wasn't afraid anymore and I was ready to be available for God and His angels to take me into the next part of my life. I claim the gift of medium ship. I am a channel to help others find peace in their lives. There is nothing to be afraid of as long as I use it for the highest good of the world I cannot fail.

"Today, God, help me be open to all my God-given gifts. I know the world is not just one-dimensional. Just because I can't see it, doesn't mean it doesn't exist. I have absolute faith when I am committed to being your instrument; I am your vehicle in action. I am the hands, ears and voice for you to move through me to complete my soul's journey and to help others find their peace and open them up to your amazing world. And, so it is."

Think it! Say it! Do it!

"Did you do it?"

How simple it is to talk about how life is going to be? Forecast your future and verbally arouse yourself. Volley the ideas around with someone willing play to the game. Express the things you want. It all sounds good. Paint the best pictures of your life.

Take a look around yourself and look at your life. Has it moved or changed? Has anything been created from those endless circling conversations? Did you do it?

If you stop and look at what you have actually created in your life as opposed to the things you talk about, you might see a trend of nothing happening at all. You just made it up. It's going on in your mind but nothing is really happening at all. Make your life move by doing something instead of just talking about it.

Honor your integrity to yourself and to others. Integrity means to be your word. If you say you are going to do something; do it. If you can't do it then make amends to the person and make a vow you will do whatever it takes to keep from breaking promises in the future.

Verbal diarrhea is an upfront way to describe the way someone spends way too much time talking about what they're going to do. Meaningless and endless words create drama in your life. They may provide the illusion that your life is complete and that the people around you may think everything is sweet.

Another way to look at integrity is to see the world as one big chain. When one link is missing the circle of support and strength is gone. Honor the chain as "one." To honor your own integrity is to honor the integrity of the all. Be your word and do it!

Think it! Say it! Do it!

"Today, God, help me become my word. Let me listen to my inner wisdom and play big in this world. I want so many things, God, but I can't seem to focus on just one thing. Show me and guide me. Let me think it, say it and then really do it this time! I release this prayer into the law of God as done. And, so it is."

Stretching

"What you resist will persist"

I once received an email from a client who did Bikram hot yoga, or as he labeled it, "Nazi Yoga." He referred to it that way because most of the time he would be very uncomfortable in class. He shared that the room was always over 100 degrees. There were 27 postures were he was instructed to hold for certain amounts of time and then repeat them. The teacher was relentless in insisting he hold the postures flawlessly under what seemed like overwhelming pressure. The point of each posture was to hold each one perfectly so he could get the benefit of each posture. Yes, sometimes it was very challenging and difficult. Each class would push him to his mental and physical limits.

What yoga taught him was that he had to deal with his body sensations and feelings. He learned to sit in the fire; sit in the burn and feel his feelings and just be with them. He would have to calm his mind down and breathe into whatever sensation he was feeling. His mind would start telling him stories like: "Oh my God, I can't hold this posture any longer. It is too hot in here. I wish I had not come today. How much longer?"

The benefits were best felt when he could hold the posture perfectly and stay in the right state of mind. When he avoided the perfect posture, the perfect hold then he was not stretching himself to evolve into a more complete person. When the going was tough it was usually because he was allowing his own mind to drive his practice.

When you allow yourself to sit inside the sensation of your feelings, pains and emotions you stretch and evolve to a level that has true holistic benefits. Within the hold and stretch comes satisfaction and only then will your soul and body connect to a higher level of being.

We as humans are evolving creatures. Without stretching and pushing forward we do not achieve our highest and best self. When we resist something it is usually a clue that we really need to move deeper into what we are trying to avoid. When we avoid something it only delays our soul's expression of who we are meant to be. When we avoid a posture or mindset we are really delaying are own peace, happiness, joy, fulfillment and greatness.

When we are uncomfortable with our lives it is our greatest awareness that we are stretching, evolving and growing. Without feeling discomfort we do not grow into the people we are meant to be. Embrace the awkwardness of strange feelings and postures that put you into a place of discomfort. Only then do you move forward, change and grow into a deeper and more fulfilled person.

Stretching is never comfortable and in yoga we learn that when you feel the stretch to the point you think you're going to tear apart all you need to do is take a deep breath and exhale even deeper. We can apply this to our lives and stretch ourselves to feel uncomfortable. From the breath we then can move more deeply into the postures of our lives. From each breath we gain an inner knowing we can move deeper and more fully into the life we were created to have.

Breathe deeply and exhale even deeper. Move, evolve, grow and expand. It's all part of God's plan.

"Today, God, help me to realize that when I am the most uncomfortable in my life is when I am expanding, growing and evolving. I know stretching is never easy and sometimes it hurts. I know now when I believe in myself and allow myself to breathe deeply into the places that stretch me the most, I will push forward and out of things that challenge me the most. I sit inside the fire today in pure and absolute faith knowing there is relief just through the breath. I release

this prayer into the law of God as done. And, so it is."

Deconstruction

"To become egoless is to become free"

If we are lucky we all go through times when we see our real selves. I know for most people it can be a trying time. When you see your real self for the first time, it can be very dismantling. You get to see all your manipulations and other undesirable character traits. You may see how you used people to get what you wanted. You see the way you move in the world and sometimes what you see isn't so pretty.

This happened to a client I worked with for years when he was isolated in a cabin in eastern Washington where he was staying in a solar-powered home on a lake. He was staying there for seven days with a friend. The plan was to have friends come and go throughout the week. At the time one of his big issues was being around other men. He had a story from his past about men being unsafe. Men in his past had always shown up in his life as bullies and creatures of destruction. Therefore, he was very uncomfortable with the thought of hanging out with other men. Here he was out of his element, isolated in rural Washington surrounded by a men's group. His normal mode of operation, which is running away and avoiding the situation, clearly was not an option this time. He was trying to act as if everything was normal with him. It wasn't; not in the least.

Within a few hours of arriving he became so afraid and confused he ran into the woods by himself and sat at the base of an older-than-God tree and cried his eyes out. After awhile he would wipe his tears and return to the house filled with men and act like everything was going fine. He would hold it together for a bit until he would virtually explode inside and return to the tree to cry. What was he crying over, you ask? Well, that was the kicker. He was crying because he was seeing himself. It was like God was holding up a huge mirror and he couldn't escape the reflection no matter where he went. It was like the sun was burning him everywhere and there was no shade; no relief in sight.

After the first day he hoped maybe he would awaken the next day to find it was all a dream. No, it was worse. He ran back to the tree to cry. He asked himself, "Why am I crying?" He didn't even really know he had any of these emotions stored up inside him. "What in the hell is wrong with me?" he yelled out loud into the forest only to hear his own echo reflect back. He couldn't get away from himself no matter where he went.

He went to the dock on the lake and found an inner tube to float on and used his hands as a paddle to make his way out into the center of this very quiet lake. He cried and cried and even there he couldn't escape himself. He remembered thinking he was being watched as he cried for his own sanity. He looked around and all he could see on the surface of the lake were little heads of turtles, sticking up poking their eyes out and watching him sit and cry while he was yelling out to God for some relief. But, it only got worse and worse.

Finally, when he became absolutely desperate he began breathing deeply into his body and exhaling even deeper. He began to visualize the in-breath as gold and the exhale as dark and blackness. "In with the gold and out with the blackness", over and over he breathed for hours. He was breathing so hard that his throat began to hurt from the friction of the air moving in and out of his throat. He was exhausted and returned to shore many hours later, only to realize he had yet to return to the cabin where his fears were waiting for him.

When he left the cabin a few days later the person he was with asked him to drive home because he was so tired. After he knew he was asleep he began to cry again. He couldn't stop no matter what he did. He really began to wonder if he was having a nervous break- down.

He drove to his apartment, got out of the car and said goodbye to his friend. He had managed to hide this episode from him and everyone else. He opened his apartment door, clicked it shut behind him and collapsed onto the floor like a pile of wet clothes.

After a few more hours of agony and crying he finally picked up the phone and dialed my number, he left me a message explaining he couldn't stop crying and needed to see me right away.

The very next morning I called and told him I was not seeing patients that day but said it sounded like he really needed to see me. I invited him to my home that afternoon. When he arrived he and I gave each other an all-knowing look, a look that expresses total understanding. He cried and he cried. He told me everything he now knew about himself and how disgusted he was with himself. He stated that he hated everything he stood for and everything he was capable of. He said he was a huge mess and needed to be committed.

With my all-knowing Yoda look I said, "Congratulations, you have finally broken through." I told him what he was experiencing was the *Deconstruction of the Ego.*

He was very perplexed with this information because he couldn't see how in the world congratulations were in order. I explained to him that he was finally seeing himself for what he was capable of. Now you can see clearly and choose to make the right choices in your life from now on.

I went on to say that I just had a 70-year-old man in my office last week that was experiencing the same thing he was. I asked him if he wanted to wait until he was 70 to really see himself? I congratulated him for being many years ahead and seeing himself at 28 years old.

He wiped his tears, blew his nose and looked up at me and said, "Wow, I am glad to see myself now rather than later. It didn't feel good while I was hurting inside, I now know it's all for the good, its all apart of my evolution."

If you ever feel like you just want to cry your eyes out for hours, days or weeks, please honor yourself where you are and allow the purging to begin. In order for you to heal you must be willing to feel. Push through the uncomfortable feelings and let it out and let it go.

When we are the most uncomfortable in our lives we are growing. My client's experience allowed him to create a new life. He is so thankful that he allowed himself to feel his feelings and learn the lessons he did in this experience.

It is easy to jump through the fire, but when we sit inside the fire and burn our butts, we do the real work.

"Today, God, let me see myself for who I am and not be afraid to see who I have become. I know through awareness I can be lifted from these awkward feelings of being raw and emotionally wide open. I know the times when I am most fragile and afraid is when I am really growing and changing. I embrace this time as part of my healing so I may transcend this place of unconsciousness forever. I release this prayer into the law of God as done. And, so it is."

React or Respond

"When you react you are co-creating with negativity. When you respond you are co-creating with God"

We have all reacted to situations in our lives in ways we now wish we had done differently. We let the negativity creep up and say things in our ears, which were not true about ourselves or someone else. We have all gotten angry, said something we regretted and hurt the people we love. We have all taken a stance or had a bad attitude at times in our lives. We may have even become righteous, blamed, harassed or made up stories, shouted, hit, verbally attacked each other, flipped each other off in our rear view mirrors or even driven by strangers in a car with looks that kill. And some do shoot to kill. These things and much more do not come from God. They come from the negativity. God is love, peace and joy.

When we listen to the negativity enough, we can come to believe the lies. When we react to our lives we move over to enemy territory and become caught in a web of illusion. Negativity divides people and causes chaos in their lives.

What do you expect from an enemy? It can be the master of deception. The enemy wants to destroy you and bring you over to its side. When you react to the things that happen in your life you do exactly what the dark energies want. You become bait by walking into the trap. You're doing all the work and the dark side gets to see a free show. The dark side or enemy wants to create havoc, drama, stress and confusion. It is it's purpose.

When you respond to something happening in your life, you take the opportunity to tune into God/Universe/Spirits mind first before proceeding. It's like having a winning lottery ticket. You take a moment to collect yourself and understand what it is you have just witnessed or experienced. You make a choice to view things with a rational mind. You move into spirits mind. You choose to experience the situation emotionally uncharged. You ask Spirit what it wants you to say or do. Taking the time to co-create with God/Universe/Spirit.

When you respond to your life you move over to a positive side and are standing below the umbrella of protection. I like to call this umbrella "God's nine fruits of the Holy Spirit coverage." It's like the ultimate insurance policy, always there, 24 hours a day.

When you stand there, Spirit blesses you with nine God-like attributes. These nine fruits are: Love, Joy, Peace, Patience, Kindness, Goodness, Faithfulness, Gentleness and Self-Control. Against such things there is no law, Galatians 5:22-24. These attributes cannot be penetrated with negativity. You are fully protected when standing below this umbrella. It's like you are inside a shark's steel cage and fully protected from harm.

Just like when you recite the alphabet you don't start with B or T. You can always beat the enemy in its game by posing an awareness question. Ask yourself this question each time something negative happens in your life,

Am I Reacting or Responding?

The answer to this question allows you to quickly see whose side you're standing on. If need be you can then make the appropriate adjustment to get back to God. At this moment you immediately cancel the enemy's plan to detour you or the other person(s) involved. The darkness can't stand the truth. So it flees to another destination to create chaos in someone else's life. When it does leave, you feel the darkness turn to light. You have won! Be aware that the enemy loves to come back to tempt you and see if you have weakened. It will always play a higher and bigger hand each time you defeat it. You are doing spiritual warfare. You must defeat the enemy and its plan to destroy you and rob you of your peace and joy.

As you continue walking in awareness and pay attention to responding and reacting you soon balance out quickly and move into a perfectly harmonious life where the enemy has no power. You have exposed negativity each and every time and plugged all the holes so nothing from the dark side can enter and destroy your life again.

"Today, God, help me to become a person who responds to my life. Help me to stay in awareness and remind me when I have walked away from your umbrella of protection. I know when I react to my life I am co-creating with negativity. I say "yes" to standing in a place of power today. I stand under the umbrella of the nine fruits and know I am fully protected from harm. I give thanks for this awareness and I know with each powerful choice I make to <u>respond</u>, eventually it will become my new normal. I release this prayer in the law of God as truth and as done now. And, so it is."

Head, Heart, Soul

"Communication with self is the first step to
having powerful relationships in the world"

As a Master Life Coach I am always working
with clients who are dealing with challenges in
their lives that need a little tuning up. Head,
Heart and Soul is one of the first tools I teach
them because it is so important each of us
understand where we are communicating from
in our bodies, which is what the Head, Heart,
Soul exercise is.

We face hectic and stressful situations
everyday. The trick is to handle them "calmly"
and "effectively" so we can be the best we can
be in each situation. I once had a friend share
with me this powerful statement, "If you are
emotionally charged, then don't go in." The tool
I am going to teach you is a great way to find out
if you are emotionally charged or not.

Imagine you are one of my clients. I would
like to describe the three levels I believe we
communicate externally and internally within our
bodies. As I describe each place in your body
please put your hand on that place.

Head- There are two sides of the brain; the left and the right. The left side is our logical side. The right side is the expressive, artistic and intuitive side. In our heads we store types of information like numbers, business ideas, directions, getting from a to b and making decisions that will move us forward in our lives in a logical linear way. Our head is a very important place to make wise and educated decisions about our lives; however, it is not a wise place to be making emotional decisions about our lives. We should only be bringing this part of the head forward when we are handling the types of things our head was designed to handle. When we are going through a break-up or handling emotional parts of our lives I would recommend you proceed to the other levels where you should be making those types of decisions, like your heart or gut level.

Have you ever had anyone tell you you're thinking too much? Well, our heads can really get us into trouble because sometimes we don't need to be thinking at all. We could stop "doing" and instead start "being." To "be" is to just be, there is nothing we need to be doing. From our heads we usually are in doing mode. Being hijacked by the insistent stream of thoughts that ping pong off the walls of your brain. It takes a little awareness to move to a higher vibration within your body. Take a deep breath and then ask the question, "What do I really know?" Don't make emotional decisions from your head.

Heart- From our hearts we communicate and connect to people, places and memories. We say in our hearts we know this or that. In my heart I know I love you. In your heart, what do you know about yourself? Do you love from your heart space? When you are making decisions from your heart remember it is from our hearts we experience empathy, compassion, sympathy, caring, admiration and devotion. These things can also get us into some emotional turmoil if we allow ourselves to be somewhat paralyzed in too much emotion which clouds our true judgment and avoids the space I call "The God Space." When you ask yourself "What do I know from the heart space?" What comes up for you? Is it connected to another person? Is it really about being connected to the person from a place of power, or is it from a place of disempowerment? If it is not about a relationship you are currently in then maybe it is about work or something else you may need clarity around. Here is an example of how our heart space can confuse us and possibly move us into a place of disempowerment.

Have you ever been in a relationship with another person and realized it was not meant to be? Your head was reacting and telling you something was wrong with this situation. In your heart you were connected to this person from a loving compassionate place where you just really didn't want to leave the relationship even though you knew it was time to go. You knew it was time to go but your head wouldn't let it happen. You just couldn't get out the words and say "GO." Why? This is where we can get derailed. Our heart space in this situation is operating from an emotionally charged level keeping us stuck in an emotionally connected place that could keep us in a state of confusion. We know it is time to leave the relationship, however something just keeps pulling us back. That something is our heart and sometimes our heart can get very clouded with reality. We want to be a good person and give each person a fair chance. Maybe they will change into the person I really want. Maybe I can help them see themselves, then when they make the correct choices I can stay with this person. Beware: The heart space is a powerful place to communicate from. However, it also has the ability to confuse us when our emotions are involved.

Knowing: The knowing space is located directly underneath your belly button in your gut. Right now place your hand directly below your belly button. Take 3 deep breaths. In and out. Slow controlled breaths. Now, I want you to hear this:

This space is where God's voice lives. It is your soul's knowing and where you can hear what you really need to be hearing. There is no confusion or chaos here, only a complete crystal clear channel of clarity you can tune into. From this space you know, that you know, that you know. It is absolute clarity and absolute truth.

This is the level you want to be making all of your decisions from. In fact, this continues into the idea that you really are responding to your life, opposed to reacting to your life.

Remember, when you are responding to your life you are co-creating with God. When you are reacting to your life you are co-creating with negativity. Awareness is always your first step. You have to be aware that you are reacting vs. responding.

This tool, "Head, Heart, Knowing" you can use yourself. Below are some questions you could ask yourself in order to define where you are communicating from.

Think of a situation in your life you would like clarity around. Once you have identified the question, place your hand on your head, heart or knowing space and then begin to take deep breaths between changing to a different position. Move through your body asking one question at time in all three areas. This process should be done slowly and calmly while waiting to hear your true voice speak. The key to this exercise is this:

Always go toward the peace within you.

Head, Heart, Soul Questions

1. Am I reacting or responding?
2. What do I really know?
3. Where should I process this information?
4. What do I need to know about myself?
5. How do I "show up" in the world?
6. What am I now willing to contribute to the world?
7. What is my relationship with the world like?
8. How can I step into my greatness today?
9. What does "walk in spirit" mean to me?
10. If not today, WHEN will I go for it?
11. How can I demonstrate trust and faith?
12. What would I do if money was not an issue?
13. Why am I angry?
14. How secure do I feel in my relationship with the world?
15. How flexible am I in relationships?
16. How am I rigid and closed off to the world?
17. How have I been pushed in a direction against my inner knowing?
18. How have I been pushed off my path?

19. What relationships still need healing in   my life?
20. What would I do if I knew I couldn't get hurt?
21. Where do I NOT speak my truth?
22. How am I willing to be independent from the opinions of others?
23. How open am I to new relationships in my life today?
24. How open am I to my own intuition?
25. What truth am I willing to speak today?
26. What do I most often worry about?
27. What am I hanging on to that holds me back?
28. What is my greatest unexpressed joy?
29. What is my greatest unexpressed sadness?
30. How much of my potential is still waiting to be expressed?

Questions from KC Miller
Toe Reading
"Are You Walking Your Destined Path"?
For a complete copy go to
www.toereadingonline.com

Exposure

"When you expose something you are hiding you take the power out of it. When you add light to something, you take away the darkness."

One day I sat with a friend who was battling a crystal meth addiction. She was telling me she was ready to give it up. I asked her how many people she had told about her addiction? "Well, I guess only you." I asked her, "Since you have been going to a therapist you must have told the therapist, right?" She replied, "No, I haven't told my therapist about my meth use."

I asked her how keeping her addiction hidden was helping her? She told me her therapist had recommended anti-depressants due to her mood swings instead of addressing her addiction to meth.

Swinging from life's highs and lows. This means one day she is happy and thrilled with life to the next day not being able to get out of bed for two to three days without drinking or eating much. When she didn't disclose her addiction to her therapist the evidence pointed to depression, which made her family feel better - her condition had a name and she was being treated with medicine. We can blame mental illness; meanwhile the addiction sees this as a perfect plan to keep the lie going.

She is actually creating more lies and more bandages to cover up the darkness and pain and the addiction is festering and becoming more and more powerful. When the pain got to be too much and she only wanted to dive into bed and sleep for days, she would use meth to give her energy so no one would see anything was wrong. She had to keep the addiction alive and protected. All the while her addiction was getting bigger and stronger and preparing to kill her.

She had also created a double-edged sword for herself because the people she worked with and her family had never seen her when she wasn't high. The happy, full of energy, multi-tasking super-woman she was when she was on meth couldn't come to work clean one day because the depressed, low-energy, mellow person might show up and then what would people think. People wanted the upbeat and high-energy person. She had to use or she wouldn't seem normal.

I began to explain to her if she wanted to kick this addiction she had to come clean with everyone she knows. She had to get honest about it. She had to expose it - take away its power. Shine a light on it. Expose it.

She looked at me like she knew I was right. She knew I was asking her to step up to the plate. I was asking her to play big. Take a risk. She had told me, now it was time to tell her therapist, her brother, a friend and her parents.

Each time you tell it, each time you expose it, it gets easier and easier. You begin to feel the power of addiction diminish. With each person you tell a number of things begin to happen. You begin to invite others into your recovery and start raising the stakes. Friends and family may hold you accountable and ask you questions keeping you talking and processing. With each conversation you have about it, more is revealed. Share your feelings and sensations with a friend for support. Ask for help and know it is ok to ask.

Take away its power. Slowly kill the lies and deceits. Pull the rug out from underneath it. Do not allow the secret to stay hidden away like a tumor deep inside a person's belly. Rip it open. Look at it. Prepare for the secret's obliteration through exposure.

"Today, God, help me look at myself with the eyes of an eagle. I know the reason I keep

things inside and hidden from others is because I am ashamed people will judge me. I make sure my life looks good on the outside when it's not sometimes! I say "yes" to the courage to expose the things keeping me from my full potential and the happiness I was born to have. I expose it now and take away its power. I take back my life and release this prayer into the law of God as done. And, so it is."

Addiction

"It's an overwhelming hunger and a pull that seems so hopeful and yet not enough to ever satisfy your deep yearning need to be filled up"

It becomes more than a want or desire. It becomes something with its own power. It's sneaky and deceptive with one intention: to get what it craves the most. It can take you over for any reason and is capable of even taking away your free will. There is a power within you that has the override switch. This power sits within you and only you have the power to override its desire.

You can fall back into your old ways so quickly with and without awareness. Slipping back is a way of revolving back to what you know. It's comfortable and securely familiar enough that it makes you feel alive and high with anticipation. The hunt almost becomes more than satisfying to your hopeful need for more validation. Have you slipped back into what you know? Going back just like a dog to eat it's own vomit?

Remind yourself you have other ways of being in the world, you are full and complete, there is nothing lacking within you. Is the addiction rising up because you are uncomfortable? Breathe through it like it's a magic wand that can take it away in one breath. Only through breathing and awareness do we expose the secret of addiction.

To transcend is to go above and move forward and away from the addiction trying to destroy you.

As I pass through the wooden double doors at Calvary Treatment Center I look down and see an embroidered carpet reading, "Expect a Miracle." At that moment I know that my mom is going to be in good hands.

I do believe in miracles and I was waiting for a sign from above that this is where my mom was supposed to land. I had been through a whirlwind of thoughts and emotions trying to figure out how to help my mom get clean from her addiction.

It had all come to a head like a pimple rising up and popping because it really needed to be addressed in an honest, healthy way. My family in eastern Washington called me, as I was getting ready to leave for a mini-vacation to Mexico with a friend. My uncle called and gave me the news my mom had just freaked out on the entire family. She cussed out my aunts and then took her suitcase on wheels and began traipsing through the snow pulling her luggage behind her. The family all went running behind her trying to stop her and convince her to stop running.

She had a demon in her eye and an attitude demonstrating she didn't want to hear or see anything anyone had to share with her. She was not looking for a solution but merely for a place to escape. She was running from accountability, responsibility and integrity. She did not want to be seen or exposed as being out of control with her drug use. She was outrageously angry at the world, confused and in a cloudy reality due to the drugs she was abusing. She was running from and into a place of complete and total denial. She was going to be right and completely uncooperative and unwilling to see the way others have experienced her and who she had become through the misuse of prescription drugs. This was going to be a long, enduring struggle because she was on the run and nothing was stopping her.

I believe she knew within herself she was being exposed because of her irrational behavior. But, she was unable to stop her behaviors because her mind and body were short-circuiting. She needed to run away from everybody because now the drugs were winning her over and everyone was watching the show. She was exposed.

She was acting like a wild animal that had just been caught in a cage. She wanted out and needed to run as far and quickly as she could. She just kept going, pulling her luggage on wheels behind her in the snow. My aunt, uncle, sister-in-law and brother were all chasing her, begging her to stop and get into the car. Nothing they were saying stopped her from running away from everyone who only wanted to help her.

My uncle, who was driving home, saw her heading down the road pulling her luggage in the snow. He pulled his car over and opened his window and asked her what she doing? When he saw her eyes all he could see was the look of a crazed person. My uncle knew what he was viewing because of his own struggles with addiction in the past. He knew she was not in her right mind. His intuition kicked in and he knew he had to approach her like the horse whisperer. He was meeting her right where she was without judgment and coaching her into the car, bringing her in slowly and allowing free choice through his powerful questioning. He was meeting her where she was and allowing her to trust him.

When she finally got into the car with him she was angry, mad, righteous, overbearing, loud and screaming out loud, "No one understands me." My uncle asked her where she wanted to go and she told him, "a motel." He drove her to the nearest motel near my family's homes. My aunt stayed with her keeping a watch on her because they were in fear she might try and do something stupid.

She lay in the motel licking her wounds and allowing my family to have some sense of control and assess the situation. They tried to figure out how to best help her with this addiction. While talking to my family I suggested they have her evaluated in a mental hospital and just see what they had to say. Once they took her in a doctor evaluated her and then quickly diagnosed her with extreme depression and released her.

My mother knew what she could say and what she shouldn't say. She made sure she worked it to best serve her. She wanted to keep up the illusion that what everyone thought they had experienced in her wasn't what it looked like. She wanted everyone to think she really wasn't addicted like everyone thought she was. I explained to my family they were not dealing with the person they knew. They were experiencing the addiction in action and she was acting out. This is part of the yo-yo effect of addiction. One thing is completely true when dealing with any kind of addiction:

Addiction is predictably unpredictable

If you are engaging with someone who is in the throes of an addiction you should remember to almost always expect there will be drama. Your job is not to get caught up in the drama. When I told my family this it seemed to give them hope and helped kick them into a higher and more powerful vibration. They transcended and moved beyond the fear and into possibility.

The next day I got a phone call from my mother's two sisters, informing me they thought I was more capable and able to help my mom than they were. They told me it was my job to get her into a recovery treatment center. They were going to put her on the first plane leaving Spokane and send her to me in Phoenix.

I was stunned because I felt like my family was dumping my mom on me. They basically told me I didn't have any choice. They felt like they had done what they could with the resources they had and now it was my turn to try. In the moment I didn't have a clue how I was going to help her. There was an overwhelming fear moving through me. All I knew to do was to breathe very deeply and respond to what I was experiencing. There was one of me and six of them. How was I going to support my life, household and daily responsibilities? How was I going to do this? "Oh my God", is all I could say. I felt overwhelmed. In this moment I looked up into the heavens and spoke out loud to God.

"God, I have no idea how I am going to do this. I am afraid this will add so much pressure to my life it might bring me down. I believe in the universe and God more than I believe in my doubt and fear. I know God, you will never give me anymore than I can handle and I now feel blessed you believe in me so much that you have given me this opportunity. God, I just ask you to give me direction and guide me through this process. I will show up and wait for you to show me the way." There is a verse in the bible that says, "Your job is only to show up when I ask for you. Don't worry about what you are going to be doing or saying because I will tell you when you get there."

I spent the next 24 hours calling all over the Phoenix valley and surrounding areas looking for direction on how to get her the proper help. I called her insurance company and found out her insurance coverage didn't cover in-patient treatment for addiction. I had to find a way to get her the proper treatment without having insurance.

After speaking with many treatment centers I found out what she would need first was a detox unit for up to six days. The detox part of her treatment was the first step and she needed to be medically supervised. There was a chance she could go into seizures and/or die. Once I heard this new information I realized how serious this was. I really got on board and eventually found both a detox unit and a 30-day in-patient treatment program. I spoke with my aunt and uncle and they committed to paying for both of the expensive programs in order to get her the professional help she really needed. I made the reservations at both the detox and treatment center and then waited for her to arrive on a plane. I had no idea what I was walking into and I don't believe she knew what she was walking into either.

This is what I call "blind faith." Walking into absolute darkness and moving forward with the faith of God. Faith is all we had to go on in this moment. I had never been through this sort of situation with anyone. I surely never thought I would be in this position with my mom. I felt like there was a role reversal and I was playing the father. Addiction takes out all of the responsibility, integrity and accountability in a person's life. So, it really didn't surprise me I was the one holding up the foundation of her life and mine at the same time.

Unfortunately, I was unable to pick her up from the airport because I had no notice of her arrival and I was scheduled to teach my usual Life Coaching class. My aunt comforted me and told me she thought my mom could take a taxi to my house and I should just leave a key to the house outside for her. It wasn't my first choice but I had to let it happen and do the best I could.

When I arrived home that evening from teaching class I found her lying on the couch in a fetal position. I walked in, slowly, and found my two dogs, Harpo and Chi Chi, surrounding her on the couch. One near her head and the other tucked up underneath the back of her legs. I spoke up and said, "Hello, mom." When she lifted her head and turned towards me I could tell she was having a hard time focusing on me and speaking a clear sentence. My thought was she probably took a whole bunch of pills as if to say, "If your going to take them away from me then I will just have to really go out with a bang."

I moved closer to the couch - almost to research my intuition and make sure I wasn't making it up. I sat down next to her and said hello again and bent over to hold her and let her know I was there to assist her in getting help. I told her I loved her and I was very proud of her for taking this step. She said she knew and thanked me for leaving the key.

I moved her to the dining room table where there was more light to see her clearly and have a conversation so I could assess her condition. What I heard from above was to "keep it simple." There was no reason to go into the story of who did what and who said what which is where she would usually want to go, defending and justifying her story and making everyone else wrong - which is another trait of addiction.

I made us a simple pizza to share and we talked briefly about her flight. Less was more in this situation and I was making sure I stayed in the now with her. She starting asking questions about where she was going and I answered simply and then moved on to something else. I shared some pictures I had taken from Mexico with her and then suggested we get to bed.

The next morning we arrived at the detox unit in a suburb of Mesa. When we walked in I immediately felt the strong, intense energy. The energy seemed to be related to pain and agony and the staff seemed a little overwhelmed. My first impression was not what I would have wanted for my mom. But, it had to be done and we had to sit in the fire.

The staff came to interview her and assess her situation. Throughout the questioning, there was much babble insinuating maybe she wasn't addicted. But every time it came up I would have to interject and redirect her to the fact she was being admitted into the unit, not released. She was really trying to paint the picture she wasn't addicted and this was a misunderstanding. She was also being very careful not to use words like *suicide* because she knew if she did she could be forced into a psych unit. Once we got through her academy award winning performance they finally established she was going to be admitted.

The staff gave her a few instructions and asked her to give them every medication she had in her bags and on her person. They explained to her before they could admit her they would have to search her and all of her possessions. She started reaching into her purse, and one by one she pulled out bottles of pills; telling a story about each bottle.

"This one is for my pain"
"This one is for my migraines"
"This one is for my thyroid"
"This one is for my back"
"This one is for my stomach"

"This one is for my IBS"
"This one is for my leg"
"This one helps me sleep"
"This one is for my headaches"

She continued to relate pills to *comfort* and a way for her to avoid the pain she was in physically, mentally, emotionally and spiritually. I once asked my mom why she took so many pills and then would pass out for days? Her response tells the true story of why. She said, "Because I want to check out."

When she finally stopped pulling out pills, the admitting nurse asked her if there was anything else in her bags. She responded with "Nope, that's it." We finally moved through most of the steps we needed to get through in order to get her admitted. The nurse left us alone so she could remove some of the things she didn't want to bring in with her. There were strict rules limiting what she could bring in. She began going through her bags and what pops out? Yes, another bag of pills. But this one was very unique because it was in a one gallon baggy. The pills in this bag were an amazing assortment of colors. The bag reminded me of M & M's candy.

"Oh, darn. I guess I forgot about these." mom commented. I wasn't convinced she really had forgotten but merely avoided that part of her bag. I took them away and then showed them to the nurse, who quickly came in and questioned her on the names of the pills. The nurse was very clear with her telling her she would be searched and that this was the time to come completely clean with anything else she may have forgotten about. "Nope, that's everything. I really did just forget about that baggy of pills. None of those are narcotics or habit forming, promise. You can call the pharmacy if you want to check and see if I am lying." She was still inside the denial of addiction.

Once she was searched and she had everything she needed for the next six days, I had to leave her in the lobby and allow her to move through the door alone. She needed to face her demons in that unit and it was time for the games to begin. I told her good-bye, gave her a hug and told her I was really proud of her and if she needed anything I was only a phone call away. She gave me a look only a mother gives her child and I turned around and walked out to the parking lot.

When I reached my car all I can remember is being in some sort of daze and confusion. I didn't feel like I was in my body. I was emotionally exhausted and I felt like the worst son in the world. I couldn't believe I had just put my mom in a detox unit. This is something I don't think you can ever prepare yourself for, and, it is the worst feeling in the world. You feel helpless and completely out of control. This is when you have a moment with God and ask, "How do I do this?" For me, this was the moment when the tears began to roll from my pressure-filled eyes and I just had to take a moment and let the tears flow and allow my emotions to be released.

Throughout the next six days I received numerous phone calls from my mom asking for medication. Each time she would call with a story. It was always about how bad she hurt and how bad her migraine was. "Please, Rich. If you just go get my migraine medicine it's the last time I will ask you. I just need a little help right now. I promise I will eventually get off of these things. My doctor said it was ok. Can you go pick up the medication from Walgreens?" The difference in these phone calls was very clear. She was detoxing hard core and feeling every ache and pain in her body, all the way from the hair on her head to the tips of her little toe nails. The tone of her voice made it sound like she was in such intense pain she didn't want to live anymore.

These phones calls were very difficult for me to listen to. Most of them were left on my voicemail because I had stopped answering her calls. I had to remember not to get caught up in the drama of it. I had to be grounded and steady. I just kept hearing this mantra run though my head:

This is not your journey anymore.

I had to let her sit in the fire alone this time. I had always had this role with my mother as her rescuer and caretaker. When I was a young boy she used to tell me everything about her life. She would talk to me about her fights with my dad and tell me things, which were none of my business. I would always go into my counseling mode with her because it seemed to work for both of us. She got to be heard and would receive great advice. I got validated for being there for her. Needless to say, she became my training ground for my profession. Even though there was dysfunction in my life, something functional happened because of it. For that I am grateful. Now it was time to break the cycle and my role as rescuer.

Throughout her six-day stay in the detox unit I kept a close eye on her via the nurses that were treating her at the time. I heard she was experiencing major difficulties and on one occasion they found her passed out in the shower, naked and unable to stand up. She had to be confined to a wheelchair from that point forward when trying to move around because she was so weak and confused. She had also experienced hallucinations and was denying herself food and liquids. Detox is only the first step to getting clean. Yes, you can remove the drugs from your system, but there is still a piece that needs to be addressed. That piece is the inner soul work. Looking at <u>why</u> you're feeding yourself these poisons.

Those six days felt like an eternity. I had to go back to my daily routine and deal with the fact that my mother was in detox and there was nothing I could do to help her. Every phone call I received I answered with a hopeful and optimistic attitude, but her asking me to get her something from the drugstore usually would ruin the moment.

I really got to see the physiological relationship she had with the drugstore. I realized this had been her life for years and a huge part of the addiction. I was having flashbacks and remembering how her daily life revolved around going to different doctors. The other part of her life was going to the drugstore to have her pills filled. It was the best part of her day and now she was being asked to let go of it.

When people have an addiction, envision this: the addiction is their best friend. They have a relationship with it daily. It is there for them anytime they need it. It has been there when they were sad, mad and glad. It has been there no matter what. It was even there when they passed out for three days and when they would awake it was waiting for them with bells on.

So by all rights you're really asking the addict to break-up the relationship with someone they love. This process takes a long time because it's just like being in a bad relationship you can't get out of. You know in your heart and soul you should leave the relationship because it is not serving you anymore, but there is something pulling you back. The addict needs time to grieve the relationship and then slowly begin to let "it" go from their life.

I got the call I was expecting on the sixth day. It was the nurse from the detox unit telling me she was ready to go. I was glad to hear it because the 30-day treatment program at Calvary was holding a bed for her on that day. I didn't want to see her lose her opportunity and not be able to go directly into in-patient treatment. It was vital she remain in constant care of professionals. She was still coming down off the drugs and was still in serious need of trained specialists.

When I arrived at the detox unit in Mesa, I waited in the lobby for her to come out. I had no idea what to expect from her. I guess I had this vision it would be like a movie where someone had a terrible stay in a detox unit and when they came out to greet their family, they would be dressed to the nines and looking like they had just been on a long relaxing, reviving retreat. Let me tell you; it was nothing like that when she finally did come out into the lobby. She was staggering, shuffling her feet and was wearing really dark sunglasses to protect her eyes from the glaring sun. To be honest - she looked tanked!

The first thing out of her mouth was "I can't do this. Do I have to go to that other f*@*+*# place?" And, of course my response was "absolutely." Again, hearing the words from above I had heard before, "Keep it simple, Rich," I asked her if she had everything and if she was ready to go. She repeated, "I can't do this." I decided to give her a really easy and achievable goal. I took her to the glass door, which looked out into the parking lot. I told her to look out and find my car. When she saw it I said, "This is the only thing you need to worry about now, getting to the car and buckling up. Are you ready?" Once we opened up the door and she could feel the sunlight on her face, I gave her a little push. Holding her up with one hand I helped her move very quickly and steadily to the car.

I knew once we got into the car it was going to be an interesting drive. She seemed very disoriented and confused. She was having a hard time understanding the seatbelt and how to insert the metal part. It almost seemed like she was behaving childlike. Once we started moving down the road I told her I had a special gift planned for her, and we were going to stop by a friend's home that was very dear to me. I needed someone who was stronger than me, someone who would join with me in prayer and pray over my mother with me. I wanted to bless her and cleanse her. I really felt I needed to make a huge impact on her. This moment was a defining moment in her life and I never wanted her to forget it.

I proceeded to tell her we were going over to KC's house. The first question out of her mouth was, "Why?" I began explaining to her that I wanted KC and I to pray over her. I wanted to protect her in her journey and seal her body and cleanse her spirit. I felt it was important she had spiritual armor for this next phase of her recovery.

When we arrived at KC's we were greeted by her lovely and warm energy. My mom knew of KC and had seen her on TV and also had taken a class from her. She didn't know what to expect; nor did I. One of KC's gifts is she really does tune into what the *Spirit* wants from her and then delivers. KC is an ordained minister and an instrument of Spirit. She was here to serve with me as spirit guides her.

We sat down for a few minutes in the living room and talked a little with mom and just allowed her to get centered and hopefully cleared from her experience in detox. I was hoping she could let go of the negativity and recharge and renew for the next part of her journey. KC ushered us into her prayer room. She had a chair sitting in the middle of the room that seemed to invite us and whisper, "Sit down here." She began introducing us to her angels, guides and statues which all had a purpose in protecting the room. KC asked my mom to sit down in the chair.

I immediately was drawn to my mother's back and laid my hands on her shoulders while KC, of course dropped to her knees and went straight for my mom's feet and toes. I closed my eyes to center myself and took a few deep breaths. I began by speaking a prayer out loud:

"Dear God,
We have come together today to intercede for my mother and friend Sandra. God, I don't have to tell you where she has been or where she is going now. We ask you to send all your angels and guides to hover around Sandra and begin with surrounding her in a protective,

peaceful, loving, soothing, calming, energy field which she may take with her into the treatment center. I know God, you have delivered her right where she is supposed to be and even in this time of confusion there is complete order and divine timing in all that is. Please watch over her and may we find her in a better place when we pick her up than when we dropped her off. In this moment I command all negativity and evil to flee in the name of Jesus. All holds and vises that may be holding on must let go now for you have no power here anymore. I claim this as truth and wisdom in the name of Jesus, the light and love of God and all his angels.

A-men and so it is."

As soon as I stopped praying I could hear my mother crying and weeping in the chair slumped over and overwhelmed. Then, suddenly KC began to pray; but this was a different prayer. She began speaking in tongues. She was chanting wildly using words and sounds I did not recognize. I trust KC so much I just allowed the process to unfold and I knew God was running this moment. KC must have chanted for over 10 minutes and the entire time she never took her hands off my mom's feet. She took the position that Jesus took when He would serve the people who came for healing. This moment was a scene right out of the bible and if you would have taken a black and white photo I am sure you would have sworn it was from that time. I almost felt like we had been transported back into a time when things were simple and everything just really seemed clear and wise. It was just pure and absolute healing energy everywhere.

Then the energy of the room changed. It felt clear and calm just like it would after a storm blew through. I knew something had changed and something had fled from my mom. All of us opened our eyes and looked at each other with a soft, optimistic anticipation. My mom was still crying with tears and sniffles coming from her body. KC asked if there was anything else we needed to pray about? Then we all sort of laughed allowing the new energy to consist of laughter and not of addiction or depression. I did speak and said I had a special gift for my mom. Both of them looked at me like it was Christmas and I had a secret gift to give.

I kneeled down next to my mom in the chair and pulled out of my pocket a small statue that used to belong to my grandma; her mother. It was one of the only things I got to keep after grandma died. I had kept it in my possession for two years. When I took it out, I knew my mom knew exactly what it was. She let out a huge gut noise of emotion. I explained to her I wanted her to take this with her to treatment. This was an anchor for her to use and remind her of the love surrounding her life. This angel represented her family and the love her family has for her. If she ever felt lost or confused or wanted to give up during her recovery, all she had to do was remember what this represents in her life. This statue was love, and then I said, "I love you, mom."

A few more minutes went by and we finally were complete. It was time to get her directly to Calvary. We said our goodbyes and appreciation to KC and moved back to the car. The first thing I noticed about mom was she seemed to be a little calmer and clearer. But, there was still something not quite right with her. She began to verbally attack me and lash out at me in a disrespectful way. I had to manage her like she was a spoiled child. She was feeling very hurt and confused and wanted me to know how bad she was feeling. "Mom, please do not speak to me like that. I am here trying to help you. I am on your side and I am not your enemy. If you don't have anything positive to say, then please do not say anything at all." Once again hearing, "Keep it simple, Rich," all I could do was drive as fast and safely as I could to Calvary.

As we stood in the lobby I noticed different people standing around talking. Most of them were wearing name badges with their pictures on them attached to a rope hanging around their necks. Everyone seemed to be talking and sharing about something. Their energy seemed to be a lot more positive and alive than when we arrived at the detox unit six days ago. We waited for someone to greet us. The first person to greet us was Frankie. She had red hair and you could tell she had a spitfire personality. "Hi," she said, "How can I help you?"

I explained we were here to check my mom into treatment. As soon as I told her who we were she seemed to know exactly why we were there. She started by asking us to sit down at a very large, round table in the middle of the lobby. There was another woman (patient) who was sitting there filling out some paperwork. When we sat down my mom immediately recognized the woman sitting at the table from the detox unit. They greeted each other with a squeal of excitement. It almost eased mom's nerves to see someone right away that she knew. My mom looked over to me and shared with me, "This is my friend from detox I was telling you about."

Frankie proceeded to give my mom the admissions paperwork to fill out. There were many, many pieces of paper she had to read, fill out and sign. Her new friend looked over to my mom and asked, "Did you know we can't talk to the men or even look at them?" She looked back to her and said, "Are you kidding me? That's not fair, that's just crap." "Yes", her friend said, "And if you get caught doing it you will be written up and after three write-up's you will be asked to leave." At that moment I knew she was exactly where she needed to be. She always had a way with the men and I am sure it was because she is a very pretty lady. Men have been very attracted to her and they were also something she could quickly focus on and become derailed from her real intention or goal. I was very pleased to hear this rule.

Once mom had finished filling out the paper-work, Frankie asked mom to put ALL her medication out on the table so she could go through each bottle dose by dose. Frankie began separating each bottle into those she could keep (non-narcotic) and those she had to dump down the toilet. Mom was pulling out all her pills, going through them one by one, the same routine as she did in detox. Story by story, excuse by excuse, just like deja vu.

For just a moment, Frankie was called back to her desk just behind where we were sitting in the same room. At the same moment my cell phone rang and I noticed it was a client I needed to talk with. I excused myself from the table leaving my mom alone with her pills and I walked out of the building to take the call. As I stood outside speaking to my client, I could see mom through a narrow window just left of the door. At that moment I witnessed her look up to make sure the coast was clear and then reach up and palm pills in her right hand and then go back to her paperwork all in three seconds flat. Acting as though she was in complete control; as though nothing had happened; she went back to her paperwork. I could feel my blood begin to boil and I quickly ended my phone call.

When I opened up the double doors I did it with a lot of power. I walked over to the table, sat down and asked her how she was doing? "Fine'," she replied, seeming very busy and into her paperwork. I sat for just a second and then began my verbal emotional tirade.

"What do you have in the palm of your right hand?" "Nothing," she said. "Isn't that funny because I witnessed you palming pills as I watched through the window." I demanded she open up her hand and let me see what was there. She was very resistant and unwilling to cooperate with me. I became aware the staff and Frankie had become very present to my conversation with my mom. The room was still and quiet and you could have heard a mouse walking on the floor. Again, with a very stern voice, I ordered her, "Open up your hand and let me see what you have in your palm." She refused me again. I reached over the table, grabbed her hand and pulled her arm straight down onto the table, pinning her down almost face first to the tabletop. "Drop it!" I exclaimed.

When she did open her palm, two small pills fell from her hand. It was like dice being thrown onto a casino table. When I saw those pills spinning to a stop, all I could feel was absolute fear, confusion and delusion. I was overwhelmed at the power of this addiction staring me in the face. I realized at that moment God wanted me to see just how bad it really was. I thought, for her to spend six days in a detox unit and then the minute it was time for her to do the work she runs back to the familiar poison – the poison that wants to kill her and take away her life and her family. It was pure insanity!

I decided it was time to play hardball with my mother and most importantly the addiction. "I am completely disgusted by what you just did. You just spent six days trying to get away from these pills and now the minute we turn our backs you go back to the pills. Here is the situation and what is going to happen now. I have done everything I can for you up to this point. I want you to hold up both palms of your hands." I placed the baggy of pills in one of her hands and the statue I had given her earlier in the day in the other hand. I explained to her she had two choices:

1   "You can continue with your addiction and continue taking pills. If you choose that direction than I have only one choice left, which is to take you to the bus station and buy you a ticket anywhere you would like to go. If you choose this option you will lose all of your family who loves you dearly. And, if you choose this option I am sure you will be homeless and dead within a year."

2   "You can let go of those pills that only want to destroy you and move through these doors and begin the work you need to do to come out a new, clean, whole person."

"What do you choose?"

In about two seconds she dropped the baggy of pills onto the floor, put her anchor into her pocket, and went back to her paperwork. I got up from the table and walked outside.

I was furious with what had just happened and what I had just witnessed. One of the staff members asked me to go outside so he could speak with me. He told me he was very impressed with the way I had just handled the situation and if every one of the families could handle their addicted loved one in the same way, the recovery rate would go way up. He told me it was normal to have something like that happen and explained that now I know how addicted she really is and how much help she really needed. Comforting me and telling me she would be all right and he advised me I should go home. I quickly went back into the lobby and I told mom, "If you don't want to stay or follow the rules of the program, don't bother me. You can just go to the bus station because you won't be welcome in my home as a depressed addicted person." I walked away and got into my car and left.

The next few days were extremely challenging for me. I had decided not to tell my family about what happened that day with mom. I knew this was a part of addiction and God wanted me to see just how addicted she really was. I had to keep it simple and not get caught up in the unpredictable drama of addiction. Telling my family would only stir up the drama and worry everyone to death. I had to transcend what I experienced and move to responding to the situation from a place of power. I just needed to leave her alone and allow the process and the journey to unfold for her and be there for her when she came out.

I had to just get my rah-rah on and get back to work. That evening I had to teach my usual Life Coaching class. I needed to walk into the class and just shake off what had just happened to me and move into empowering my students. I did an amazing job because I was in my soul and humanness and this is where my passion comes from to teach powerfully.

About one week into her treatment I got a call from her asking me if I could pick up some items from the store. She rattled off a list of the things she needed that had been approved by Calvary. She was unable to leave the treatment center for the first few weeks and had no car or anyway of getting to the store. I decided I would call ahead and make sure it was ok for me to get these things for her. The staff confirmed the items were approved so off I went to the store.

I arrived at Calvary Treatment Center late that evening walking through the double doors over the embroidered carpet announcing, "Expect a Miracle." Each time I walked over the carpet I felt my soul and body vibrate at a higher level. I knew this was where she was supposed to be. A woman I had never seen before greeted me. She asked if she could go through the bag of things I had brought in. She went through each item one by one and then handed me back the can of Aqua Net hairspray and said no aerosol products were permitted in the center. She asked me to go and sit at the round table in the middle of the room, then got on the intercom system and paged my mom.

While I sat and waited a *miracle* crept up and sat down in front of me. A young man around 19 wearing shorts came over and sat directly in front of me as though he knew me. I wasn't quite sure why he had just taken space in this counselor/client position. I said hello to him and he said, "Hey, what's up?" I asked him his name and he told me it was Jason. I introduced myself and then looked down at his right leg to see his entire leg had been mutilated and shredded with a lot of scar tissue everywhere. His leg looked like it had been put into a shredder. At first it almost took my breath away and I had to adjust to the sensation I was experiencing. Of course, like always, I had to ask him the question, "What happened to your leg?" He began telling me a horrible but amazing story.

"In High School I was a track star and I got a scholarship to Penn State University. My life was going somewhere and I felt excited about its possibilities. One day, when I was home, I decided to go for a run down the highway near my house. I had run this same course hundreds of times so I was very comfortable with the route. I was running on the right side of the road going with the flow and direction of the traffic. As I ran I was swept into an 18-wheeler's front trailer axel. I was spun through seven sets of tires and then spit out like a rag doll from behind. When I was found, they airlifted me into town and thought they might have to take my leg off. I went through months and months of recovery and skin grafts and rehabilitation. After I got home I went into a mega depression and wanted to die. I was so angry with God for letting this happen to me. I was desperate so I turned to drugs and alcohol. Now I am here trying to get back on track and reclaim my life."

I was just sitting there stunned; unable to speak any words. I am sure my mouth was hanging wide open and I looked blown away. I realized in a flash something huge had just happened because my body was quiet. I again looked down at his leg and in a flash I saw the message loud and clear.

Jason's leg represented a clear view into what the soul of an addicted person looks like. An addicted person's soul is mangled, shredded, torn-up and looks abused and in very bad shape. They have been sucked in and spit out the back end. This is what addiction is, abuse to self, spirit and body. I was amazed to have the ability to see the message and that I had just experienced a miracle. I knew God had delivered Jason to me that night.

In perfect timing I looked up to see my mom coming down the hall. I thanked Jason telling him it was nice to meet him. "Blessings and may God be with you," I told him. I stood up and greeted my mom. We went outside and talked near the fountain. We had a stressful, hard conversation. She was emotionally wide open, raw and really feeling her feelings. She needed to tell me about her treatment and what she was learning. During the time we spent together I was feeling very guilty and I needed to leave before she pushed me too far. I knew I was becoming emotionally attached and I needed to go. She was screaming at me and saying I always run away. I responded to her by saying, "I can't handle seeing you like this right now - a bleeding wound who needs to be healed." Hearing God say to me, "This is not your journey anymore," I told her I had to go and left her sitting on the bench.

I didn't see her again for almost 2 weeks after that visit. I was still very mad but also I knew a miracle had taken place at the same time. I received a call from her counselor, Ann, requesting I come in and have a meeting with her and mom. She was going to be graduating in a week from the treatment program and they wanted to talk about her discharge plan.

The meeting between us went very well and my mom was back to normal. Her eyes were clear and she was speaking clearly and rationally. She was owning up to her wrongs and talking about what she had learned about herself. We also established our relationship needed some cleaning up. Ann explained to both of us that I had to stop rescuing mom and my mom needed to find herself and her own friends and couldn't rely on me for her emotional support. She needed to get healthy and begin creating her own tribe of friends who would support her. I was sometimes her surrogate husband. In order for her to move on and find a healthy relationship, we had to detach in a healthy way. We both agreed with Ann and we acknowledged we needed to heal our relationship.

A week later mom was released from her program. She had successfully graduated from the program and when I picked her up I could tell she was a new person. I opened the door for her to walk to the car and said, "Welcome to your new life." She stepped outside and over the embroidered carpet "Expect a Miracle." A miracle happened for us and I am sure there will be many more to come for Calvary. As she walked to my car, she did so with power, purpose and without resistance. She was a new person and how grateful I was to receive this gift.

My mom is now living in Washington State. She is surrounded by her two toddler grandkids, Cole and Rysa, who have very powerful positive influence for her. She has remained clean for

240 days and is now working at an active retirement community as an activities coordinator and teacher. Her position at the retirement community was God sent. She is now helping the elderly find their purpose everyday. In return, it has given her a reason to continue living a drug-free, purpose-filled life. She is doing very well and taking each day one day at a time. I know she will continue to blossom in her life without fear or drugs to mask her feelings. She is completely living in the now and is being very truthful and open with her relationships. She is a miracle and I am so proud of her.

"Today, God, I live each day moment by moment knowing I can be drug-free and clean. I know when I am scared or unsure of myself I can always find comfort in sharing my life with you. I know I do not need to cover up my feelings or emotions. I can expect a miracle each and everyday just by being aware and open. I say "Yes" to my life and the miracles it holds for me as a sober and amazing child of God. I release this prayer into the law of God as done. And, so it is."

Blessing in the Storm

When I cannot hear the sparrows sing.
And I cannot feel the melody.
There's a secret place that's full of grace.
There's a blessing in the storm, help me see it now!
There's a blessing in the storm.
And when the sickness roams,
I want to leave my body.
And the pain just won't leave my soul.
I get on my knees and
I say Jesus please.
There's a blessing in the storm,
help me see it.
There's a blessing in the storm.
Oh why?
When I cannot seem to love again.
And the raindrops won't seem to end.
If you just hold on those clouds will soon be gone.
There's a blessing in the storm. Help me see it.
There's a blessing.
There's a blessing. Oh, there's a blessing.
Yes, there's a blessing in the storm.
There's a blessing in the storm.
-Kirk Franklin

Revolve or Evolve

"If you don't go within, you go without"

Do you ever get the feeling your life is going in one big circle? Well it may be. Let me paint a picture for you of how it might look if you stood back and looked at the situation from a higher perspective.

Start to float upward toward the sky and notice everything immediately seems to get smaller. Higher and higher you go until you're so high you can see for hundreds of miles all around. You look directly below from where you came and what you see blows you away. Hundreds of long, narrow, winding tubes on the ground, all going in different directions. North, south, east, west and everywhere in between. In the middle of it all you see a 12-foot circle with a path going out to the outer edge that is worn deeply into the earth. Some of the paths leading to the tubes appear to be more worn down than others. You're perplexed in seeing this because it seems so limiting. You notice the tubes are labeled, each one marked somewhere near the top. You descend toward the earth getting close enough to each tube to read:

Addiction, Love, Relationships, Family Issues, Detachment, Money, Job, Isolation, Cyber- addiction, Commitment, Smoking, Security, Drugs, Drinking, Debt, Abuse, Neglect, Sex. The list can go on and on.

What does your tube say?

From your vantage point, I ask you to become a nonjudgmental observer. You are calm and at ease. Look at the tubes and their labels. Which one has cost you the most in your life? Look and reflect back and listen to your inner knowing. Which one is the most terrifying for you? Which one makes you nervous and makes you want to run away? Is there one that is the "big" one?

Once you have identified the tube that has created the most fear for you, start flying above it and follow its direction. Slightly tilt your body forward and move yourself along the tube and follow it's path. Take your time and move along noticing any negative emotions associated with the tubes contents and let those feelings pass by. You are calm and graceful as you float along. As you go further and further, you see the tube turns, bends and becomes wider or narrower in places. You notice there are places where there is no light and the tube is extremely narrow and you wonder how anything could squeeze through. Ahead you notice the tube is coming to an end. On the other side of the exit is a large area with green grass and lots of light. You become relieved because you realize there is a place outside of the dark tube that is free and open. It is a beautiful peaceful place for you to expand run and grow.

Now you have a choice. You now know from your angelic perspective the tubes end with a happy ending, You now know you will come out the other side of the tube to a pleasing, happy place. Float down now; back to the circle. When you land, understand the challenge before you is to travel through the tube of your greatest fear, if you choose. Choose which tube you will enter. Just take a moment and get centered by taking in three deep breaths. If you are ready, move ahead keeping your eyes fixed forward on the light to guide you to safety.

With each footstep you take there may be darkness and confusion. There may be anxiety and fear or some other emotion. Whatever does come up for you, remember the tube you are in has an end. There is relief at the end. There is an exit if you just keep moving. Don't let the fear of the unknown frighten you and cause you to go back to the circle. Your goal is to push forward so you can release yourself from the pain you have been in. Move through your tube with the faith of God. This is how you grow. We

tend to delay our own evolution and expansion by continually revolving back to what we know, back to the entrance to the
tube - a place which may be uncomfortable but familiar. Now you have seen the truth of the matter.

With each tube we successfully walk through we open and expand our circle. As we exit each tube, it closes behind us and we know we never have to travel through it again if we choose not to. We no longer need to fear the dark narrow spaces; we no longer need to avoid them. There is no freedom in avoidance, only a delay in our peace and joy.

By not walking through those tubes of your life you keep yourself from expanding your life. You keep yourself in a state of unconsciousness - a continuous circle that keeps revolving and never moving away from.   The truth is what sets us free. The truth is there is always an end to the misery. God gives us nothing we can't handle. So, the choice is up to you.

Do you want to revolve or evolve? You choose.

"Today, God, I give up my attachment not to evolve. I am walking through my tube today with the awareness and faith of God. I know there will be a light to guide me to the end of

this tube. I begin to walk forward knowing God has my back and this is only a demonstration of a made-up illusion in my mind. I release this into the law of God as done." And, so it is."

Gratefulness

"The quickest way to manifest anything you need in your life is to be grateful for what you have now"

Sometimes it is difficult to be grateful. Some of us may say to ourselves, "How can I be happy and grateful when my life isn't going the way I want it to? What do I have to be grateful for?"

One day I received a call from a friend who explained to me she was feeling like her life was filled with doom. She was thinking about how many things she didn't have and how horrible her life was. She was focusing on the negative aspects of her life and playing the poor me victim. She was mentally telling herself all the things she didn't have and all of the things that were going wrong in her life. It was a total downhill spiral from there. As she shared with me she began to sink deeper into a self-induced coma of negativity. She just seemed to keep sinking deeper and deeper into all the things that were wrong. She couldn't find a way out of the hole.

After living a life of negative focus she started to creep back to the light when I asked her a simple, but huge question that changed everything for her from that day forward:

"Tell me what you are grateful for today."

She shared with me she is grateful for her home, life, health, music, her mind, friends, awareness, God's angels that surround her, God's love, her breathe, the air she breathes, her relationships, the water she drinks, her animals, her car, her family, her job and much more.

She began to realize she did have a lot to be grateful for. We continued to ponder the question and she started to realize, slowly at first, God was supporting her all the time. She just didn't know it. She shared with me she was never taught to see the morning dew that shocked the bottoms of her feet in an early spring morning of the northwest as a blessing and a gift from God. She began to realize being alive and having the experience of the dew on her feet was a blessing. The more she became alive to the many good things happening all around her the more grateful she was. Her life transformed before my eyes with one simple question.

From that day forward she committed to practicing this new idea. And the more grateful she was the more her life went the way it should.

Of course there were times when she would lose her gratitude and slip back into the cracks of negativity. But she learned to start praying to spirit for guidance and for Spirit's lessons. When she would ask for help she was awakened to what is possible and came back with a punch of gratitude, ready to push negativity away from her life. Spirit's energy was always there to support her. Within just seconds the clouds would lift and like an aspirin kicking in there was relief and then passion and joy.

After many months of experiencing the same results we decided to give it a name so we could share this as a tool for other people to break through. I call it the *Grateful process*. A way to release you from your own personal hell!

Instead of looking at your life like you have nothing, start seeing what you already have and start being grateful for what is coming to you now. God is always there for us and is ready to do what we tell it to do. It is God's inherent nature to do for us. Spirit energy is the ultimate doer of our lives. God is a doing machine and only knows to do what you tell it to do. The fastest way to change our state of mind is to be in absolute gratitude for our lives. Start with the simple things like our breath moving through our lungs, your heart that beats without interruption.

Here is how the process works: Get up every morning and set your intention for the day. Intention is everything, and without intention we are wandering aimlessly without a plan.

"Today, my intention is to see my life as abundant and thriving. I am willing to see that even in my negative perceptions of things that even in this God is present. I am willing to see through the eyes of love and apply love in any situation I encounter."

The intent or goal is to see everything you experience in your day through the eyes of love, as good and positive because Spirit served it up. Seek to find the spiritual lesson in all things. Be grateful for your life lessons. You can start by being grateful for a multitude of things. If you would, at the end of this chapter, make a list of everything you are grateful for. Throughout the day revisit the list and read it out loud.

As you walk through your day remember your intention and keep the focus. Stay focused on what you have and see through the eyes of love. As you start to practice the *Grateful process* you will begin to start filling up with abundance and you will begin to feel positive energy moving through you and all around you.

In my experience, when I practice being grateful, eventually I am so full that I am overflowing with positiveness and God's abundance and I begin to "bliss out" and burst forth into love and gratitude. As you go through your day being positive and grateful you will see how people are drawn to you like moths to a light. Most of them will not know why they are drawn to you, but you will. It's an awesome experience and it is a very powerful tool.

The reason this process works so well is because God loves to give more when you appreciate the gifts you receive. Think of it as a spoiled child. Have you ever been around children who were so spoiled that nothing was enough for them? The child had many toys, stuffed animals, clothes and amazing surroundings but the child couldn't see or appreciate it. The child has so much, but having never been without and never been taught gratefulness it is hard for the child to be grateful.

When I am around children who are spoiled my tendency is to stop giving and instead teach them to value what they have. I know in the child's eyes everything is temporary and undervalued. Even the small things are overlooked. If I meet children who are grateful and appreciate what they have my tendency is to give more. God is exactly the same way with us because we are His children. God likes to be acknowledged for the things He does for us. When we see what we have in life now then our life transforms before our eyes.

Even in your darkest hour, God will always love you no matter what. God will never leave your side. If there is a time you cannot be in gratitude for your life and appreciate your gifts, this is when you should get on yours knees and start praying for gratitude. Spirit sees you as magnificent, full and complete; there is nothing lacking within you. God/Universe/Spirit loves when you see your gifts. Spirit will continually be by your side even when you cannot be there for yourself. Eventually, through absolute faith and prayer you will find your gratitude again and come back to the light and your many gifts.

" Today, God, help me become a more grateful person. Help me realize when I am depressed and only seeing the negativity in my life all I have to do is look around and I will see you everywhere supporting me all the time. I am willing to start being grateful for the smallest things today. I begin by being grateful for my life. I am grateful now. I release this prayer into the law of God as done. And, so it is."

Ultimate Sharing

"Love is Transmutable"

The place we call earth is an amazing cosmos of laws wrapped in the idea of love. No matter what is going on in your life, any hurt, pain, abuse, fear, poverty or suffering can be cloaked and surrounded by a veil of love. The condition you are experiencing dissipates like a puff of smoke.

Love is the ultimate way in which we can share ourselves with other people. Love is something that should be given without expectations or attachments. Love is absolute truth and purity without poisons or viruses moving through its core. Love is one thing in this world that cannot be destroyed or taken away. We can keep it in our hearts and minds without the risk of losing it.

God yearns to love us. He is always waiting for you to share yourself with Him. When you come to Him at the 4 a.m. hour He is usually the only one up at the time to visit with. He sits with bated ears of love wondering what it is you could share with him. He is like a proud grandfather who only gets to see his children once in awhile. He says to you, "Come my child, sit and be in communion with me. I want to have a relationship with you. Talk with me and share your life with me."

You can always go to God to share yourself; you are never separated from your higher power. You are always being supported all the time. Sharing is the ultimate way in which we can be connected to each other and God. When we connect and share ourselves with another person it's like God is sitting in the middle of our conversation being the ultimate facilitator. There is magic inside sharing, there is love inside sharing, love is transmutable and interchangeable and never can be destroyed.

I invite you to continue this journey as a human with the protection and armor of love; the protection of sharing in love is the ultimate weapon against any condition in this world. Wrap anything in love and watch the miracle of a word called love move and change everything in a second. To love is to share and to share is to love. It is the ultimate sharing with God that produces and transcends all negativity. Become anchored inside the idea of communion with a loving, powerful, all-knowing, divine presence.

Step up - tune into a higher powerful vibration for the most spectacular

communication you can experience. Share your
God-given gifts with the one Divine mind moving
through you and all around you. God wants to
hear you, see you and help you. God wants to
enrich your life. It all ends in God.

It all ends in love if you choose.

Conclusion to Addiction
Authors Update: 3/01/13

In the chapter called *Addiction* I shared very candidly about my mother's struggle with addiction and how it affected my family and I personally. Since the 1st edition was published back in 2007 I have received hundreds of emails from people all over the world; sharing with me how much the *Addiction* chapter helped them comprehend and cope with their loved one who was or is addicted.

My mother was completely involved and overseeing the writing of the addiction chapter in this book. At times, she would read it and call me and say, "Really, Rich, did that really happen like that?" There was nothing I could say, but, "Yes, mom, it did. But, what matters now is that you are healed, clean and living a sober life."

My mom always wanted me to write a conclusion to the chapter. Where I left off in the book was that she went to work for a retirement community serving elders living in an active retirement center find purpose everyday. This was her major struggle in her life; finding a purpose after her kids left the nest. And, of course, as I teach, we teach what we need to learn the most.

This was the key to her sober survival after she left treatment. Having something to do with her life everyday, waking up with a purpose. My accountability to her was to keep her talking, communicating and letting her know I was there and supporting her.

One day I had a very unmistakable significant knowing. I knew I was supposed to go visit my mom. I instantly booked a plane ticket on line, and then called her to let her know I was coming to see her the following week. This was very uncharacteristic of me; because normally I would have called first to make sure it was a good time to show up for a visit. But, on this day, the clearest knowing I can ever remember having, came over me. I was shown a vision to go be with her.

We spent an astounding five days together, doing what we did best. Chatting, sharing and drifting around going wherever we felt like going. We visited with family and the little ones and really had a very relaxing unforced visit.

On the very last day of my visit I was planning to stop by to see her before I headed to the airport. When I arrived at her house the door was open, the sun was shinning into the house and I heard music playing inside the house. I recall feeling so united to the energy that was streaming from the house. I walked through the open door, heard her upstairs in the bathroom, music playing, her singing and doing her hair. I could hear her spraying hair spray onto her hair, I knew this sound internally because it was a sound I have heard all my life. I decided to just take in this moment and sit down on the couch and breathe in this moment.

I sat good-naturedly, engulfing the moment, scrupulously enjoying the feeling. I was calmed by this undemanding moment in time, a moment in time that I have had thousands of times before, but this seemed unusual, I could not put my finger on why it felt out of the ordinary.

She walked down the stairs and when she turned I shocked her and she did her normal screech and saying, "Damn you, why do you always have to scare me! How long have you been here?" "Hi mom, I have been here about 20 minutes. I've been sitting here enjoying myself and listening to you get ready for the day. "What's so pleasurable about that?" She replied. We both snickered and she sat down in the chair across from me.

There seemed to be something else in attendance during the next two hours we spent together. The exchange was very deep, ingenuous and being guided by a very encircling wise energy. I recall as if there was no time at hand and that we were in a very significant divine moment.

As we talked something she said to me still echoes back to me today. I had told her how proud I was of her to contemplate going back to school to broaden her education. Her reply to me was, "I don't know, Rich. I just don't think I am going to be here for much longer." "Oh, mom, don't say that. You have a lot to look forward to and you just turned 60. You could have 20 to 30 more years." She just looked at me with a very apprehensive glare in her eyes.

It was time for me to leave and catch my plane home. She walked me outside, we hugged, we cried, hugged some more. I got into my car, rolled down the window and she looked directly into my eyes and said, "Let me come back with you. I have nothing here; I could start my life in Phoenix. I just feel I am ready to try something new and if you could let me live with you for awhile, it will give me time to find a job and get back on my feet." I remember the surprise, and the self-centeredness that came over me. Here I was a full-grown man in the primary part of my life and my mother lives with me? I just couldn't envision my life functioning effectively with this as my reality. I replied with, "Mom, everything is going to be completely all right, you have your grandkids and family here.

Besides, Phoenix is a big city and I do not think you would do well there. I am always just a phone call away." With eyes full of snuffle coming from us both, I unhurriedly drove away and headed towards the airport.

Twelve days later on May 30, 2009 she went four wheeling with my uncle on a beautiful spring day. Four wheeling is in my family's blood and my mom has ridden thousands of times. I used to kid her because she was able to outride my brothers and I easily. Mom was one of the people who taught us how to ride.

My uncle and mom rode to the summit of a local mountaintop. They sat on a flat rock overlooking the Spokane Valley and enjoyed a sandwich and drank a bottle of water. After about an hour they decided to head back down the mountain so they could get the four wheelers loaded and get home before dark.

They slowly made their way down the hill following an old logging trail. My uncle was leading the way and would verify in his rear view mirror as they journeyed down. Each time he would glance into the rearview mirror he would see my mom riding along and enjoying herself. She was just taking in the sites and splendor of the forest. He then glanced back and didn't see her anymore, he looked to his left and saw my mom bearing straight down a very sheer forested hill and losing control of her four-wheeler. In a millisecond the four-wheeler flipped and landed directly on top of her and she was killed instantaneously.

I cannot tell you how this calamity has affected me and how I function in my life. My life has never been the same since. There is a very deep hole within me that nothing can fill up. I miss her everyday, and wish I could have had just one more conversation with her. I have friends who have lost their parents to slow killers like cancer and sometimes I have felt like I was cheated the chance to spend one last day with my mom. However, I know how self-seeking this is, because those friends, who have lost their parents to slow killers, wilted away, lost their spirit and became feeble, weak, delicate and frail. The agony and quality of their parents lives in the end is beyond words. I would have never chosen for her to wilt away and slowly disappear.

My mom, *Sandi Delores Seaman* died sober, happy and doing something she loved doing - four wheeling. We know she was liberated from drugs and living clear-headed, because there was a mandatory autopsy performed by the state. She was clean and sober as she transitioned, going back to the Divine, the source of her true happiness.

In Memory of:
Sandra Delores Seaman
3/29/1949 – 5/30/09

About the author

Richard Seaman is the founder and director of Seattle Life Coach Training and one of the nation's top spiritual authors. A native of Seattle, Richard teaches and trains people to become successful transformational life coaches.

He has been a Master Life Coach and motivational speaker for more than 17 years. With his wise and intuitive knowing, and uplifting and straightforward approach, he has coached and guided thousands of people to a more powerful, passionate life. He continues to grow a very successful life coach training program in Seattle, WA.

Richard also teaches at the Southwest Institute of Healing Arts in Tempe, AZ. Arizona's award winning, private holistic healthcare college, and Seattle Life Coach Training in Seattle, Wa. Richard was awarded the ***"Best Teacher of the Year 2011"*** by the Arizona Private School Association.

Richard is the author of the book: *It's All in the Sharing and It's All in the Sharing – Companion Journal. Spiritual Reliability* (soon to be released), which helped secure a spot for Richard as one of America's next top spiritual authors.

SEATTLE
LIFE COACH TRAINING
train to transform lives
www.seattlelifecoachtraining.com